WHISPERS ALONG THE MISSION TRAIL

Whispers along the Mission Trail

GAIL FABER and
MICHELE LASAGNA

MAGPIE PUBLICATIONS
ALAMO, CALIFORNIA

Dedicated to the brave men and women of yesterday and today whose dreams have inspired us and continue to inspire us to search and find and know
and
the California Indians who built the missions that are now a part of our California heritage.

ACKNOWLEDGMENTS

The authors give special thanks to the following persons for their particular contributions to this book:

Father Virgilio Biasiol, Don DeNevi, Sharon Marocchi, Judith McCarty, Harold Smith, Pat Weik and Allen, Tina and John.

First Edition August 1986

Published by Magpie Publications
        Box 636
        Alamo, CA 94507

ISBN: 0-936480-03-3 Student soft cover edition
ISBN: 0-936480-04-1 Student hard cover edition
ISBN: 0-936480-05-X Teacher edition

Dear Reader,

As you read this book, you will explore with many brave explorers. You will meet courageous men and women who dared to follow their dreams in spite of many uncertainties.

Your explorations will begin with Columbus' journey to the New World in 1492, almost 500 years ago! You will sail up the coast of California with Cabrillo, Vizcaíno, and other famous sailors who searched for California harbors. You will explore with daring men who blazed new trails into the uncharted lands of California. You will meet the California Indians who shared their golden land with others. You will journey with the Spanish padres who dedicated their lives to the beautiful missions of California. You will be there when the missions are built, one by one along the *El Camino Reál*.

As you journey, think about the people who came to this land long before you. Let the whispers of these brave people help you discover a special part of your California heritage!

The Authors

TABLE OF CONTENTS

WHISPERS

The shore of the beautiful California bay was bustling with activity. A tribe of Indians had made their yearly trek to the coast from their home far beyond the mountains. For many days Indian men and boys had fished in the blue waters of the bay. Their nets and spears brought them many fish, enough for the long winter ahead. Indian women and girls dried the fish over smoky fires and packed the dried fish in large burden baskets. Soon the tribe would be ready to travel the long trail back to their home.

As everyone worked, a warm breeze blew over the bay. The waves splashed on the shore and noisy gulls circled overhead watching for a chance to snatch a scrap of fish. The setting September sun painted the skies crimson and soon the busy day would be over.

Suddenly a loud cry of warning pierced the air! An Indian boy perched high on a cliff above the shore was shouting and pointing to a rocky point of land that jutted out into the bay. As everyone watched, a great winged creature rounded the point of land, its huge white wings billowing in the breeze. Everyone stood in silence. Even the gulls quieted and flew to the nearby cliffs to watch.

As the great winged creature came closer, strange sounds could be heard — clanking, rattling, and then a loud splash as something very heavy was dropped into the waters of the bay. The creature stopped. Men's voices could be heard. They spoke a language unknown to the Indians. Soon, men wearing strange clothing left the great creature and began rowing small boats toward the shore.

The Indians gazed in wonder at the men in small boats who were fast approaching the sandy beach. Who were these men? Some of the Indians began to wade out into the water to meet the first Spanish explorers to sail into a California bay. Little did the Indians know that as they met these explorers a new chapter in California history was about to begin!

Astronaut Bruce McCandless II is testing a new unit that will give the mission specialist more freedom of movement in space.

CHAPTER ONE
NEW WORLDS TO EXPLORE

EVERYONE IS AN EXPLORER

People have always liked to search for new lands, places, and ideas. People who like to search for something new are called **explorers**. Perhaps you are an explorer and have discovered many things in your neighborhood or a friend's neighborhood. You can be an explorer in your own home. At home, you may explore ways to make your life easier, such as inventing a fantastic machine to do your chores! Sometimes exploring can lead you to the shopping center, the park, a campground, or a creek. At one of these places you may discover a new friend, a hobby shop, or a hummingbird's nest. You may find things that have already been discovered, but are new to you such as a forgotten trail or some very old Indian grinding rocks.

Exploring is fun, but sometimes can be hard work. Men and women work many long hours exploring ideas to make our lives easier. Aren't you glad scientists have explored and discovered polio and measle **vaccines**? Aren't you glad that inventors have explored ways to send pictures and sound through the air with television and radio? Global explorers have sailed from ocean to ocean, journeyed from **continent** to continent, and space explorers are exploring planet to planet! It is in everyone's heart to search and find and know!

Dr. Sally Ride was born May 26, 1951 in Los Angeles, California. She graduated from Stanford University with a doctorate degree in physics. Dr. Ride was selected as an astronaut by NASA in January, 1978. In June, 1983, Dr. Ride joined four other astronauts and made her first trip into space as a mission specialist. The mission lasted 147 hours before landing at Edwards Air Force Base in California.

Astronaut Kathryn Sullivan, mission specialist, is learning how to use space equipment so that she may explore new worlds in outer space.

CHRISTOPHER COLUMBUS

An explorer you already know about is Christopher Columbus. In 1492, Columbus, a bold sea captain, had an exciting plan. He had studied many maps and knew much about seas and ships. He believed the world was round and that he could sail west across the Atlantic Ocean to reach Asia. Columbus wanted to find a new way to reach Asia. He wanted to bring silks, jewels, and spices back to Spain. The King and Queen of Spain gave Columbus money and three small ships called **caravels** to sail across the Atlantic Ocean.

Columbus prepared for a trip that would be much like a trip that the astronauts would take today. Columbus, however, did not have **navigational** computers, a **communication** system, or jet engines. He had only the wind to blow the sails of his three ships and the stars to guide him. Columbus was just as brave as any of our astronauts today and he was anxious to sail into the unexplored world.

Columbus did not reach Asia. He reached a group of islands in the Caribbean Sea and claimed them for Spain. Columbus thought he had reached the Indies, islands off the coast of Asia, but instead he had reached the islands in the Caribbean Sea near the continents of North America and South America. He had discovered the **New World**.

Brave Christopher Columbus made several trips to the New World and his journeys caused much excitement in Spain. Columbus is important because he discovered the New World and his bravery encouraged other explorers to journey to the New World.

In 1492, holding a sword and the flag of Spain, Christopher Columbus claimed an island in the New World. He thought he had reached Asia.

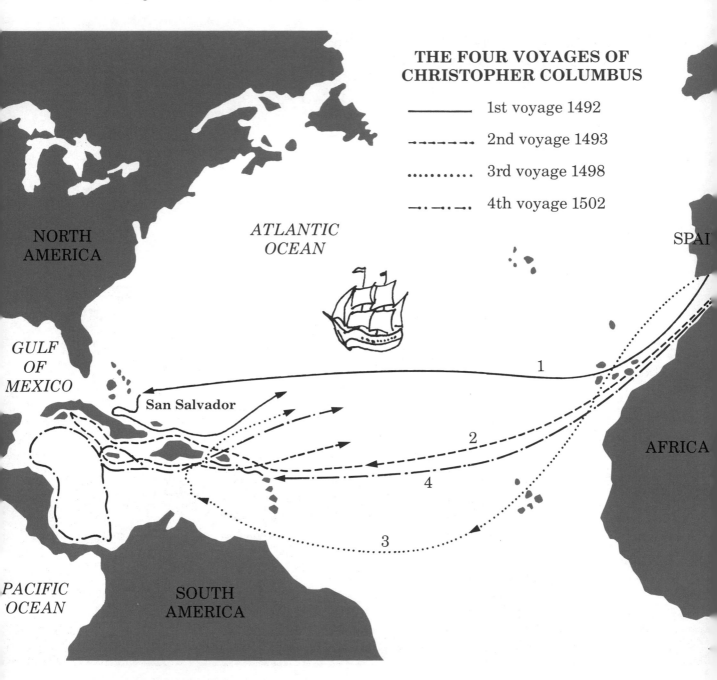

THE FOUR VOYAGES OF CHRISTOPHER COLUMBUS

——————— 1st voyage 1492

– – – – – – 2nd voyage 1493

············ 3rd voyage 1498

—·—·—·— 4th voyage 1502

NORTH AMERICA

ATLANTIC OCEAN

SPAI

San Salvador

GULF OF MEXICO

AFRICA

PACIFIC OCEAN

SOUTH AMERICA

1

2

4

3

Christopher Columbus made four trips to the New World. Each time he returned to Spain he brought with him some of the things he had found in the New World, such as tobacco, sweet potatoes, and colorful birds.

Columbus' idea of sailing west from Spain to reach the East Indies *was* correct. What Columbus did not realize was that two huge land masses called continents lay in his path.

THE FIRST VOYAGE AROUND THE WORLD

Ferdinand Magellan, another sea captain, wanted to finish the search that Columbus had started. He wanted to find the East Indies off the coast of Asia by sailing west. In 1519, the King of Spain put Magellan in charge of five ships. The ships were filled with food and clothing because no one knew how long the voyage would take. Magellan left Spain and sailed across the Atlantic Ocean to the continent of South America.

After many months, Magellan found, near the southern tip of South America, a water passage leading to the Pacific Ocean. This water passage is now called the **Strait of Magellan**. Magellan sailed through this water passage and out into the great Pacific Ocean. His sailors begged him to return to Spain, but he would not turn back. Magellan had promised the King of Spain that he would find the East Indies. "We will go on until the sails rot and the ships fall apart," Magellan told his men. "We will go on even if we have to eat rats and the leather in the **rigging** of the ships!" They did go on and unfortunately his words came true. They did eat rats and leather!

After crossing most of the Pacific Ocean, Magellan eventually reached the islands that are today called the Philippine Islands. Magellan claimed these islands for Spain. Magellan was killed in a battle with some natives on these islands, but many of his crew were able to sail on to the East Indies, around the southern tip of Africa and home to Spain. Magellan's crew and the one remaining ship, *Victory*, had made the first voyage around the world!

MAGELLAN'S TRIP AROUND THE WORLD, 1519

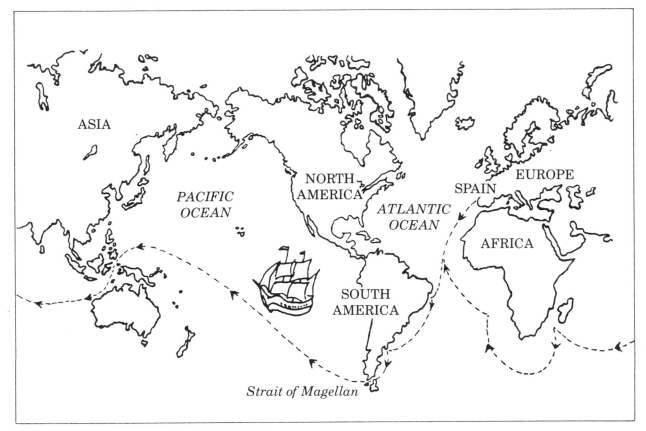

The around-the-world voyage of Magellan's ship, *Victory*, in the years 1519-1522, clearly proved that Columbus **had** discovered a New World. It also ended forever the old belief that the world was flat.

EXPLORATIONS OF BALBOA AND CORTÉS
IN THE NEW WORLD

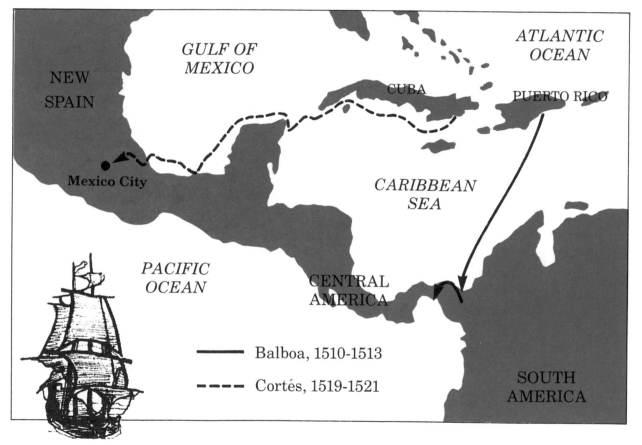

Hernando Cortés, a Spanish explorer, came to the New World in 1519. With over 600 men, Cortés marched into what today is the country of Mexico. He fought and conquered the Aztec Indians. The King of Spain made Cortés the governor of New Spain.

Vasco Núñez de Balboa was an adventurer and an explorer. He left Spain and came to the New World soon after Columbus. Balboa and his men crossed the narrow neck of land that today we call the Isthmus of Panama. They were the first Europeans to see the Pacific Ocean from the New World.

CHRISTOPHER COLUMBUS

I, Christopher Columbus, have always loved the sea. As a young boy, I spent most of my time at the docks in Genoa, Italy. I watched the sailors load and unload the ships and I listened to the stories they told. Some of the sailors believed that the earth was flat and that if a ship sailed too far out to sea, it would fall off the edge.

As I grew older, I studied many maps and talked to many scholars who believed that the earth was round. I, too, believed that the earth must be round and I also believed that if a ship sailed west it would reach Asia.

After many years, I finally convinced the King and Queen of Spain to give me ships and money to sail west to find a new route to Asia.

I set sail on one of the bravest voyages that a man or woman has or ever will undertake. With ninety men, I left Palos, Spain in August, 1492. I had three caravels, the *Niña*, the *Pinta*, and the *Santa Maria*. I set the course due west.

During my voyage, I kept two logs. One log was for my crew to read. It showed the ship's position for each day at noon. The other log was my secret log. In this log I kept track of **nautical** miles. I did not want my crew to know how far we were from Spain because some sailors might be frightened and cause a **mutiny**.

I was so sure that these islands were off the coast of Asia near India that I named them the Indies and the people who lived here I called Indians.

I returned to Spain and the King and Queen were so pleased with me that they honored me with my own coat of arms. They told me that they wanted to send Spanish settlers to these lands to build Spanish cities. The King and Queen told me that because of my discovery, Spain would one day be the most powerful country in all of Europe.

Now, after several voyages to San Salvador and the surrounding islands, I am still unable to find the mainland of Asia. I am beginning to wonder if these islands are, indeed, near Asia. Perhaps, I have discovered a land no one has ever seen before. Perhaps, I have discovered a New World!

One day, after many weeks at sea, I saw a group of seagulls. I decided to follow them because I knew they must be flying in the direction of land. I was correct! On Friday, October 12, 1492, land was sighted! We had reached a group of islands. We landed on one of the islands and I raised the Spanish flag and claimed the land for Spain. I named the island that we stood upon San Salvador.

BACKTRACKING

1. Why is it important that some people in this world are explorers?

2. What was Christopher Columbus' plan?

3. Why was Christopher Columbus' journey important?

4. What did Magellan find near the southern tip of South America?

5. Name two **characteristics** that Columbus and Magellan had in common.

6. What did Magellan's voyage prove?

BRAVE EXPLORERS

1. Name three explorers you learned about in this chapter. Tell why each was important.

This statue of Christopher Columbus and Queen Isabella is in the state capitol building in Sacramento.

Cabrillo and his crew were the first explorers to sail along the coast of Alta California. Cabrillo is honored by many statues, parks, schools, and streets. A marine museum, a national historical monument, and an annual music festival also honor Cabrillo.

CHAPTER TWO
CABRILLO'S CARAVELS

SETTLERS IN THE NEW WORLD

The discovery of the New World brought glory to Spain. More explorers became interested in exploring the New World. They searched for gold, silver, and other riches. Soon much of North America and South America was claimed by Spain.

Hundreds of Spanish people came to the New World and lived in New Spain or what is today called Mexico. The Spanish people built cities as beautiful as the old cities of Europe.

Padres came to New Spain. They learned the Indian languages and built **missions** in New Spain or what is today called Mexico. The padres wanted the Indians to live and work at the missions. They wanted to teach the Indians the **Christian** religion, farming, and the European way of life.

The King of Spain sent officers and a new governor to rule New Spain. The governor, called a **viceroy**, was the most important man in the government of New Spain because he **represented** the King of Spain. The viceroy sent news and letters to the king to keep him informed about what was happening in New Spain.

JUAN RODRÍGUEZ CABRILLO

In 1542, the governor of New Spain, Viceroy Mendoza, was ordered by the King of Spain to send explorers northward along the Pacific Coast of North America. These explorers were to explore the Pacific Coast as far north as they could in search of good harbors. They were also to search for a river that would connect the Pacific Ocean and the Atlantic Ocean. The Spanish called this **fabled** river the **Strait of Anián**.

Viceroy Mendoza put a brave Portuguese leader named Juan Rodríguez Cabrillo in command of two caravels, the *San Salvador* and the *La Victoria*, on this ocean expedition. Captain Cabrillo was a skilled **navigator** and a capable captain for the **rugged** adventurous sailors of that time. Many of Cabrillo's crewmen were convicts from Spanish prisons. Bartolomé Ferrelo was the chief pilot and second in command of Cabrillo's expedition heading north along the Pacific Coast of North America.

THE DISCOVERY OF SAN DIEGO BAY

Cabrillo and his sailors sailed from Navidad, a little town in New Spain, up the coast of **Alta** or **Upper California** and anchored in a beautiful bay that today is known as San Diego Bay. It took Cabrillo and his men three months to sail to this fine, large harbor and here they met and talked sign language with several Indians. Little did Cabrillo know that the first Alta California mission, Mission San Diego, would be **founded** here two hundred years later.

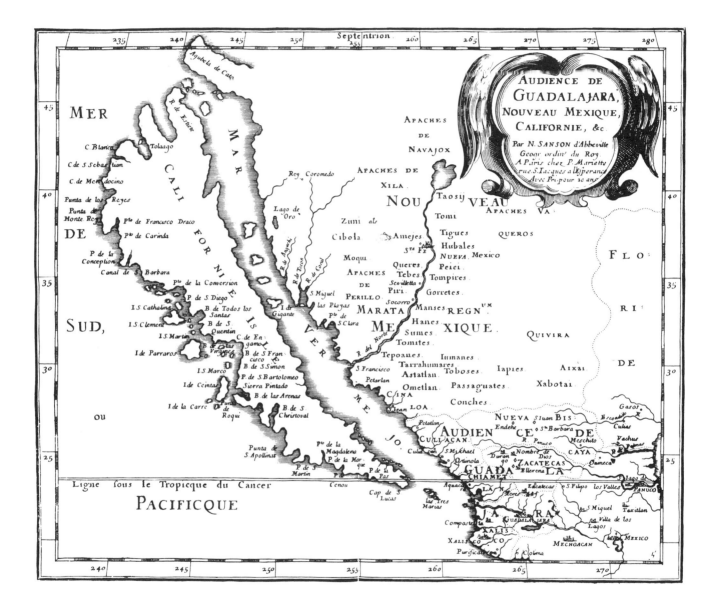

It is not known how California got its name. When the early Spanish explorers came to the land we now call California, they thought it was an island. They named it California because they remembered a story by Ordoñez de Montalvo that told about an imaginary island ruled by a queen named Califia. Perhaps it was for this queen that California was named. Another explanation of how California got its name comes from the Latin word "califaco" which means warm.

SAILING ALONG THE COAST OF ALTA CALIFORNIA

Cabrillo, his men, and the caravels, *San Salvador* and *La Victoria*, continued their exploring journey charting landmarks, measuring depths of the ocean, and exploring north along the Alta California coast. From the deck of his caravel, Cabrillo noticed clusters of tule huts on the shore and so many Indian cookfires that he named the area the Bay of Smokes. This area is now called Santa Monica.

Cabrillo's caravels then sailed along the coast that today is called Santa Barbara. Cabrillo watched as welcoming parties of Indians launched their plank boats and rowed out to greet the caravels. Cabrillo's sailors were impressed with the Indian craftsmanship of these fine boats. It must have been an interesting journey for Cabrillo and his men as they met the native Californians and explored California by sea.

AN ACCIDENT

During a storm, Cabrillo's ships were forced to take shelter on one of the small **Channel Islands** off the coast of Santa Barbara. It was here that Cabrillo fell and broke his shoulder. In spite of his great pain, Cabrillo did not turn his ships back to New Spain, but continued sailing north along the coast seeking safe harbors and a river to the Atlantic Ocean.

As Cabrillo and his men continued their journey, they saw what looked like a good harbor. The harbor was surrounded by pine trees, but they could not land because the waves were too rough. They named this harbor the Bay of Pines. Today, many people think this bay was Monterey Bay.

When Cabrillo landed at Ventura in 1542, he named the site El Pueblo de las Canoas for the remarkable canoes that the Chumash Indians rowed out to meet his ships. These plank canoes could hold as many as twenty people and were navigated by men kneeling on the bottom of the boats using double bladed paddles.

After further explorations northward and needing
a rest, the men sailed back to the Channel Islands
near Santa Barbara where Cabrillo died of blood
poisoning from his broken shoulder. Cabrillo's pilot,
Bartolomé Ferrelo, carried out Cabrillo's last orders
and commanded the caravels to sail as far north as
they could still searching for the undiscovered water-
way to the Atlantic Ocean which the Spanish called
the Strait of Anián.

SCURVY STRIKES!

On Ferrelo's voyage many of the men grew sick
with **scurvy**. This was a terrible disease that was
caused by lack of fresh food, especially fruits and vegetables. The sailors with scurvy were unable to stand,
move or eat. Their gums swelled, their teeth loosened,
their legs turned purple, and their muscles grew stiff.
Many sailors died of this disease. Ferrelo could not go
on. His caravels were forced to sail back to Navidad in
New Spain.

BRAVE SAILORS

Although Cabrillo and Ferrelo did not find the
water passage to the Atlantic Ocean, the Strait of
Anián, they had done much for Spain. Wherever Juan
Cabrillo or Bartolomé Ferrelo had gone ashore, they
had claimed the land for Spain. They had discovered
one good harbor and liked the land and warm climate
of Alta California. They had sailed north to what is
now the state of Oregon and proved that Alta California was a great mainland and not a group of islands.

BACKTRACKING

1. Why was the viceroy important to the King of Spain?

2. Pretend you are a California Indian living on the coast near Santa Barbara. If you rowed your plank boat out to meet Cabrillo, what might you think of Cabrillo and his large ship?

3. Pretend you are one of Cabrillo's sailors and you are greeting the Indians in their plank boats along the Santa Barbara coast. What do you think of these Indians and their boats?

4. Why were the Spanish looking for the Strait of Anián?

5. What causes scurvy? Do sailors on ocean trips today suffer from scurvy? Why or why not?

6. Why was Cabrillo's journey important?

BRAVE EXPLORERS

1. How do you think Cabrillo communicated or talked to the Indians?

2. Look up scurvy in your encyclopedia and find out who found the cure for this disease. Draw a picture to go with your story.

After the year 1565, the Spanish began sending the Manila Galleons from New Spain to the Philippines once a year. For the next 250 years the Manila Galleons sailed from Manila back to New Spain laden with cargos valued at millions of dollars. Manila Galleons were never safe from attack and several were captured by pirate ships. Many of these large heavy loaded ships were lost at sea due to storms and rough seas. People today still search for sunken treasure from these Manila Galleons.

20

CHAPTER THREE
TRADE WINDS AND SEA DOGS

SPANISH SHIPS SAIL TO THE PHILIPPINES

After the voyages of Juan Rodríguez Cabrillo and his crew, the Spanish became interested in other explorations. The Viceroy of New Spain sent Spanish ships across the Pacific Ocean to explore the islands in the **East Indies**. In 1543, they found the group of islands that Magellan had discovered in 1521 on his voyage around the world. The Spanish named the islands the Philippines in honor of Prince Philip, the son of the King of Spain.

THE MANILA GALLEONS

Ships sailed from the town of Acapulco in New Spain across the Pacific Ocean to the Philippine Islands. The ships were called **Manila Galleons** because they sailed to Manila, the capital of the Philippine Islands. Sailing *to* Manila was fairly easy because of the **Trade Winds**. The Trade Winds are steady, strong winds that move with the spin of the earth and always move in the same direction.

In the Philippines, the ships were loaded with silks, jewels, spices, gold, ivory, and other treasures.

Returning *from* Manila, back to New Spain, the journey was more difficult because the heavily loaded galleons were going *against* the winds. Ships were overturned by the wind and waves and many sailors drowned.

HELPFUL WINDS

At last a sea captain, exploring the coast north of the Philippine Islands, found that the wind filled the sails of his ship and moved his ship northward along the coast of Japan and then the wind blew his ship eastward across the Pacific Ocean to the California coast. Upon reaching California the winds again filled the winglike sails and blew the ship southward to New Spain. The discovery of these Trade Winds helped the Manila Galleons, but the return voyage from the Philippines to New Spain was still long and hard. Sea captains wished that they could find safe harbors on the Alta California shores because the sailors needed a place to rest and get fresh food and water on their return journeys from the Philippine Islands. The Spanish sea captains wondered, "Could a harbor be found farther north than the one Cabrillo had found at San Diego Bay?"

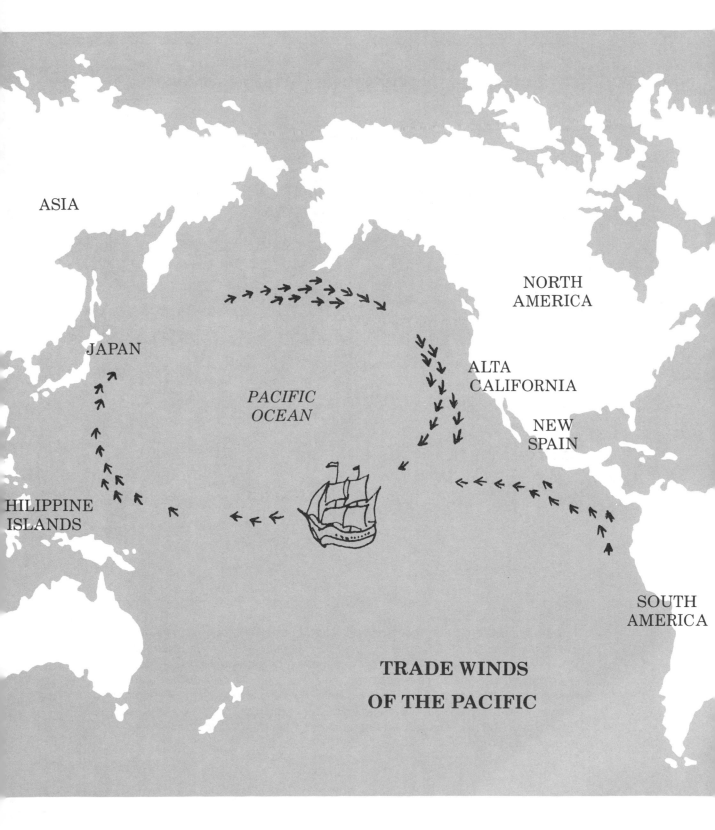

ASIA

NORTH
AMERICA

JAPAN

ALTA
CALIFORNIA

*PACIFIC
OCEAN*

NEW
SPAIN

HILIPPINE
ISLANDS

SOUTH
AMERICA

**TRADE WINDS
OF THE PACIFIC**

ROUTE OF THE MANILA GALLEONS

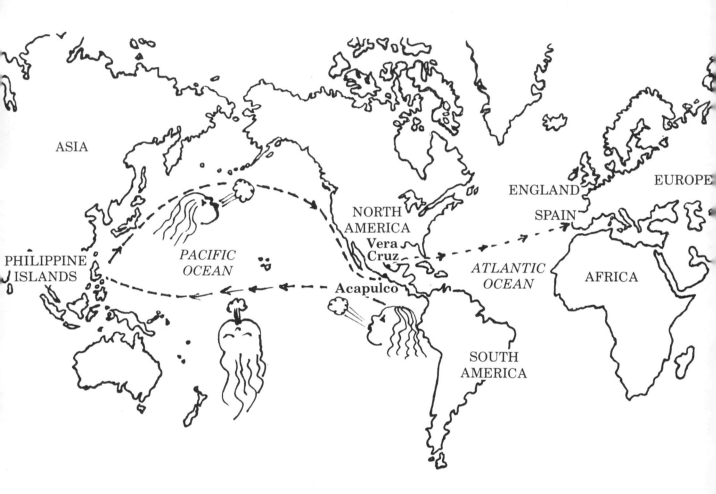

The Manila Galleons left Acapulco and sailed to the Philippine Islands where they were loaded with treasures such as gold, jewels, ivory, silks, spices, etc. When these ships returned to Acapulco, they were unloaded and the goods were packed on mules. The mules carried the goods on the long journey across New Spain to the port city of Vera Cruz. Here, the treasures from the Philippine Islands were taken off the mules and loaded aboard ships that sailed to Spain. From Spain, the silks, spices, and other riches from the Philippines were sold throughout Europe.

FRANCIS DRAKE

During these years, Spain was the strongest country on the Atlantic and Pacific Oceans. Other countries, such as Portugal, Russia, Holland, France, and England also wanted to rule the seas, but England was Spain's most feared enemy.

A daring English sea captain, named Francis Drake, attacked and **plundered** Spanish ships at every opportunity. Drake and his men were called "sea dogs". They were proud of this name because they took treasure as a dog would steal a bone. They dashed into battle against the treasure ships of Spain, defeated them, took their **cargos** of treasure, and sailed quickly away.

In 1577, Drake, on his flagship, the *Pelican*, led four English ships across the Atlantic Ocean to the coast of South America. There he unloaded and destroyed two of his ships because he knew that the journey ahead would be difficult and these two older ships were not seaworthy. During a dangerous journey through the Strait of Magellan at the tip of South America, Drake lost contact with his two remaining ships. Drake and his sailors on the *Pelican* found themselves alone on the Pacific Ocean. Here, he changed the name of his ship, the *Pelican*, to the *Golden Hind*.

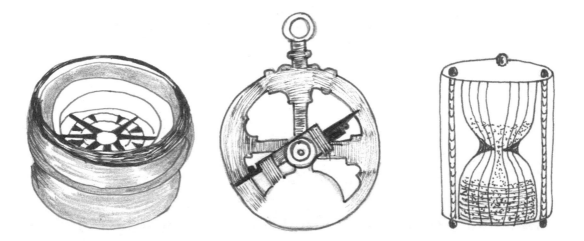

On board each caravel was a binnacle or small box with a compass in it. The needle of the compass always points North. An astrolabe measured the sun's distance above the horizon and gave the North-South position of the ship. This is all that the sailors had to steer by. A sand clock measured the time and looked like an hourglass.

Drake sailed northward on the unguarded Pacific coastline that led directly to the Spanish treasure city of Acapulco. Drake found it easy to **raid** and **seize** great amounts of gold and silver as he sailed up the Pacific coast. He caught the Spanish by surprise because the Spanish never expected to see an English ship on the Pacific Ocean. Drake also robbed the Manila Galleons as they returned from the Philippine Islands.

Drake knew the Spanish would be waiting for him if he returned to England by the Strait of Magellan, so he continued sailing north along the Alta California coast looking for a water passage to the Atlantic Ocean. When he couldn't find the fabled Strait of Anián, the link between the Pacific Ocean and the Atlantic Ocean, he knew he would have to sail across the Pacific Ocean to return to England.

DRAKE'S BAY

Drake's ship was so heavy with treasure that it could hardly sail and before setting out across the wide Pacific, Drake and his "sea dogs" dropped anchor at the place we now call Drake's Bay, north of San Francisco Bay. Drake stayed there for more than a month, cleaning the **barnacles** from the bottom of the *Golden Hind*. Drake also explored the land. Before he left California, Drake called the land **New Albion**, an old name for England. He claimed California as an English **possession** on behalf of Queen Elizabeth I.

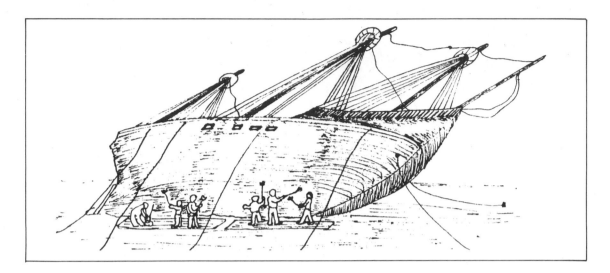

After one year at sea, Drake's ship, the *Golden Hind*, was careened or tipped over in the shallow waters at Drake's Bay. The ship was careened by carefully shifting the heavy cargo to one side of the ship. The crew spent several weeks scraping the barnacles off the bottom of the ship and caulking the leaky seams.

The picture of these two ships makes it easy for you to understand why life at sea was so much more dangerous long ago than it is today. A large steamer like the one in this picture is more than three hundred times as large as the little ships that were used to explore the coast of Alta California.

When Francis Drake landed in Alta California in 1579, the Indians thought that he was a great spirit. They brought him gifts and necklaces and crowned him as their chief. Drake stayed thirty-six days and claimed the land for England.

Three years later when Drake returned to England, he told everyone about the beautiful land of California that he had claimed for the Queen. Drake wanted to bring settlers back to California to build an English town. Now, the Spanish had two reasons to further explore California. They needed to find safe harbors for the Manila Galleons and they needed to keep the English from building towns in Spanish territory!

FRANCIS DRAKE'S VOYAGE AROUND THE WORLD, 1577-1580

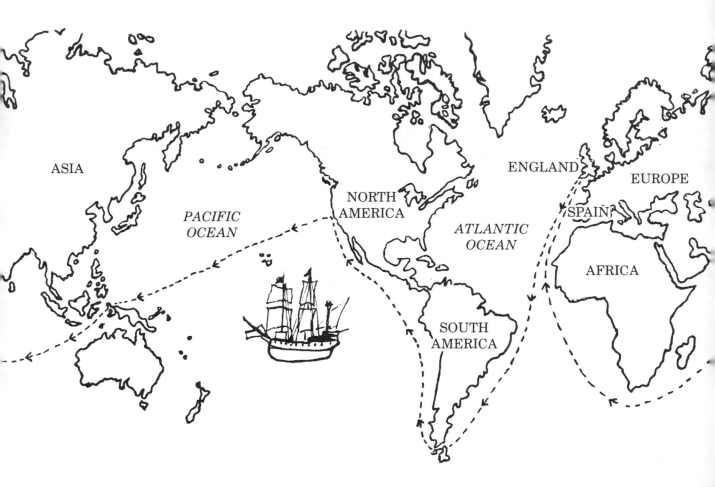

Drake sailed around the world in 1577-1580. He was knighted by Queen Elizabeth I in 1580. Drake's explorations along the Alta California coast made the Spanish government realize that it must send settlers to Alta California in order to keep the land out of England's grasp.

BACKTRACKING

1. How were the Trade Winds both helpful and dangerous to the Manila Galleons?

2. At this time in history, why was Spain so powerful?

3. What country did Francis Drake represent? Why were Drake and his sailors called "sea dogs" and why were they proud of this name?

4. Why is Francis Drake important in California history?

BRAVE EXPLORERS

1. What kind of guns do you think were used when the Spanish and English ships fought? Ask your school librarian for references or check an encyclopedia.

2. Look up Francis Drake in an encyclopedia. Where was he born? Tell about his young life. How did he become "Sir" Francis Drake?

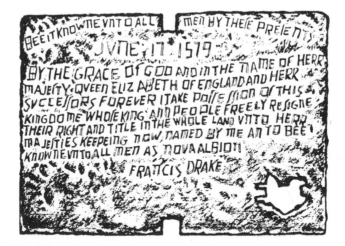

During his trip around the world in 1579, Francis Drake anchored in a harbor in Alta California where he remained about a month to repair his ship, the *Golden Hind*. To prove that he had discovered and claimed land in Alta California, Francis Drake nailed a brass plate to a post stating that the land had been claimed for Queen Elizabeth.

About fifty years ago, a metal plate was found on a hill overlooking San Francisco Bay. At first, many people believed this was Drake's plate. Later, scientific studies showed that what was thought to be an ancient brass plate was not a piece of brass that would have been used during Drake's time.

Many years ago there were huge herds of sea otters along the coast of North America from California to Alaska. The otters lived in thick beds of seaweed near the shore. Because of their beautiful fur, these animals were hunted and killed until very few were left.

CHAPTER FOUR
CRUEL SEAS AND COURAGEOUS SAILORS

EXPLORING WITH THE GALLEONS

The people of New Spain heard about Drake's adventures along the California coast. They also heard that he had claimed the land for England and planned to build English towns along the California coast. This news upset the Spanish people and so the King of Spain asked the captains on each of the Manila Galleons to explore the coast of Alta or Upper California on their return trips from the Philippine Islands. The Spanish sea captains were to look for harbors that would give protection against the English ships that might come into the Pacific Ocean.

The Spanish ship captains found that exploring the California coast with their galleons was very difficult. The Manila Galleons were very large and heavily loaded with treasures from the Philippine Islands. The ship captains were afraid to sail too close to the rocky coastline of California for fear of smashing their ships on the rocks and losing their cargos.

RODRÍGUEZ CERMENHO

Rodríguez Cermenho, the captain of a Manila Galleon, was ordered to explore the California coast on his way home from the Philippine Islands. His galleon was heavily loaded with precious treasures from the Philippines. Captain Cermenho sailed his ship as close to the rocky coastline as he dared, looking for a good harbor. One morning, as the galleon sailed around a point of land, a beautiful little bay was sighted. This bay had been discovered by Francis Drake many years before. While Cermenho was anchored in Drake's Bay, a storm came up and huge waves smashed Cermenho's galleon on the rocks. The galleon was destroyed and most of the cargo was lost. The Spanish officials realized that the Manila Galleons were too large and too valuable to explore the California coastline. Plans were made to send smaller ships to California to explore for good harbors.

It was difficult for the large galleons to sail too close to the rocky shores of Alta California.

No one knows exactly how the galleons looked. Old stories tell us that these ships were very big. These galleons with their guns and large cargo spaces were built to sail the high seas and carry heavy treasure.

SEBASTIÁN VIZCAÍNO

In the year 1602, the Viceroy of New Spain sent for Sebastián Vizcaíno, a bold sea captain who had sailed many times on the Manila Galleons. The viceroy decided to send Captain Vizcaíno to Alta California to find a port and to search again for the Strait of Anián. Sailors, soldiers, Carmelite padres, and a mapmaker went with Vizcaíno on this important voyage.

Vizcaíno set out in May of 1602 with three small ships sailing north along the California coast. He followed the same **route** that Captain Juan Cabrillo had taken. As he traveled, Vizcaíno's mapmaker **charted** the bays, islands, and capes along the California coast.

MONTEREY BAY

Vizcaíno sailed on up the coast and came to the beautiful harbor Captain Cabrillo had originally named San Miguel. Vizcaíno renamed this harbor San Diego. Further north, he found a large harbor bordered by pine trees. Was this the Bay of Pines that Cabrillo had seen many years before? In this bay, Vizcaíno found a place to anchor and discovered streams and rivers with fresh water. He also noted in his ship's log that there were many pine trees on the shore for building ships. He found the Indians there friendly and helpful. He felt this bay could become a safe harbor for the galleons returning from the Philippine Islands. Vizcaíno named this harbor Monterey in honor of the Viceroy of New Spain, the man who had sent Vizcaíno on this voyage.

Vizcaíno sailed farther north to Drake's Bay, but his sailors were suffering terribly from the cold weather and scurvy. Without further explorations, Vizcaíno and his **weary** crew, too weak and ill to look for good harbors, sailed back to New Spain. Perhaps, because of their illnesses and the heavy swirling fog, the sailors did not see the narrow gateway leading to the greatest harbor on the California coast, San Francisco Bay!

REPORT TO THE VICEROY

Sebastián Vizcaíno told the viceroy that Monterey Bay would provide a good harbor for the Manila Galleons and also be a good place to start a Spanish town. The viceroy did not pay attention to these ideas because he felt the trip to California was too long, hard, and expensive.

For more than 160 years no Spanish ships sailed into California harbors. During these years, however, other countries such as France, England, and Russia began to show more interest in the New World.

THE RUSSIANS ARE COMING!

Around the year 1745, Russian sailors sailed across the Bering Sea and started a settlement in Kodiak, Alaska. The Russians were hunting the valuable fur of **sea otters**. The Spanish heard about these explorations and were worried that the Russians would build a **permanent** town beside one of California's fine bays. If the Russians moved into California, who would own California? Now, King Carlos III of Spain began to worry that other countries might try to take over the lands that Cabrillo and Vizcaíno had already claimed for Spain. He wrote a letter to the Viceroy of New Spain saying,

There are Russians on our northern shores. We must keep them out of California. We must build Spanish towns in California. These towns will protect our galleons and show other countries that Spain has claimed this part of the New World

Carlos III
King of Spain

BACKTRACKING

1. What treasures did the Manila Galleons bring from the Philippine Islands?

2. What was difficult about exploring the California coast with a galleon?

3. Why was Vizcaíno sent to Alta California?

4. Why was Vizcaíno important to California history?

5. Why was the King of Spain upset by the Russian hunters on the California coast?

BRAVE EXPLORERS

1. What do you think would have happened if Russia or England had claimed land and established settlements in Alta California? What would it be like in California today if this had happened? What language would we speak?

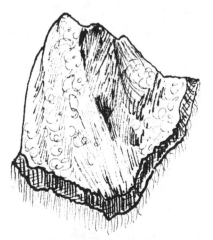

One of the stops Sebastián Vizcaíno made was on the island of Santa Catalina. He saw Indians wearing skins of deer or rabbits. One woman appeared in a shawl of Chinese silk. Vizcaíno knew that the shawl had come from China. He felt that perhaps it had come in Cermenho's galleon. Vizcaíno believed that Cermenho's galleon was wrecked on the northern shores of Alta California. Indians had found the shawl. They traded it from tribe to tribe. The shawl had come all the way from the northern bay to Santa Catalina Island off the southern shores of Alta California.

Father Serra was one of the first padres to come to Alta California. Spanish soldiers came with him. This bronze statue of Father Serra is in the Capitol Building in Washington, D.C.

40

CHAPTER FIVE
A DECISION IS MADE

A PLAN FOR EXPLORING AND SETTLING ALTA CALIFORNIA

José de Gálvez was the King of Spain's special **representative** to New Spain. He traveled throughout New Spain, inspected the lands and towns and sent reports back to the King of Spain. One day Gálvez received an **official** letter from the King of Spain that said:

if we want to keep the Russians out of California, we must build a town there. You are near California. You must make plans to send an expedition of Spanish people to California

King Carlos III

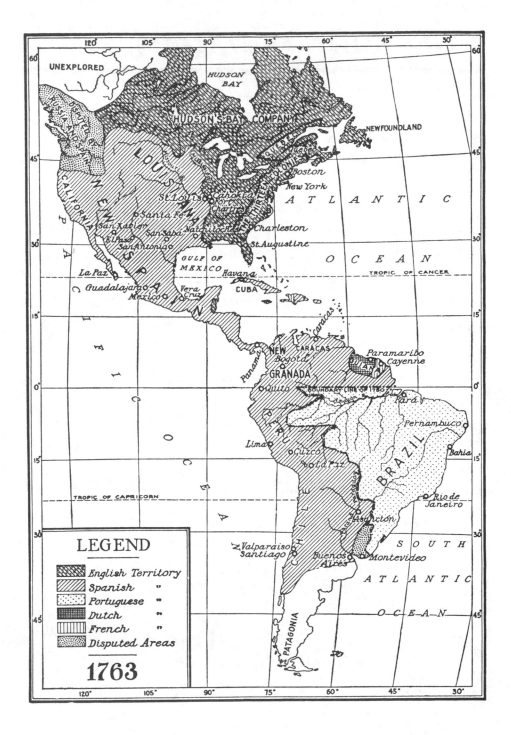

The Americas in 1763

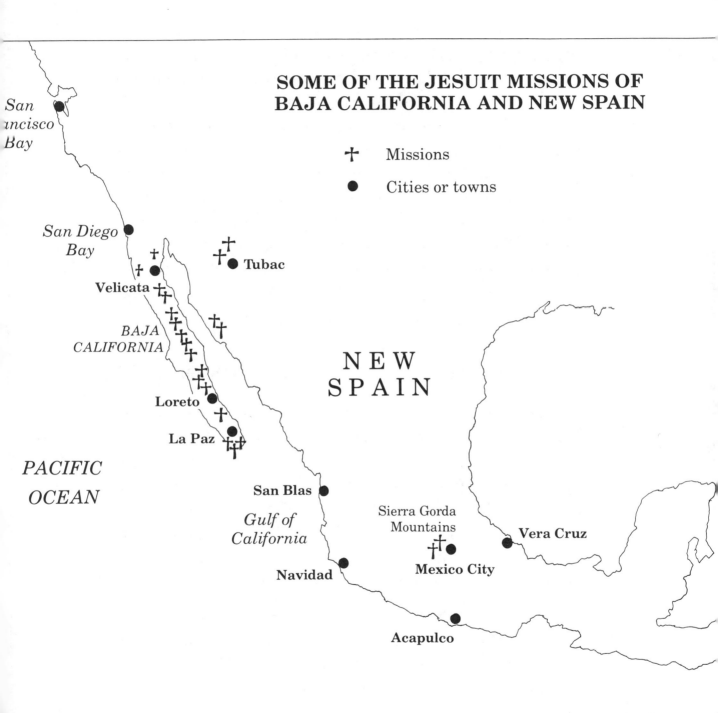

**SOME OF THE JESUIT MISSIONS OF
BAJA CALIFORNIA AND NEW SPAIN**

✝ Missions

● Cities or towns

*San
ncisco
Bay*

*San Diego
Bay*

Tubac

Velicata

*BAJA
CALIFORNIA*

*NEW
SPAIN*

Loreto

La Paz

*PACIFIC
OCEAN*

San Blas

*Gulf of
California*

Sierra Gorda
Mountains

Vera Cruz

Navidad

Mexico City

Acapulco

This map shows some of the many missions that the Spanish built in New Spain
and Baja California before they started missions in Alta California. Father Serra
was the president of all the missions in Baja California from 1767 to 1769.

Gálvez thought about all the problems there would be to send an expedition of Spanish people to Alta or Upper California. Gálvez carefully studied the maps made over 160 years earlier by Cabrillo's and Vizcaino's mapmakers. After a great deal of planning, Gálvez thought about sending both sea and land expeditions to Alta California. He knew large numbers of men would be needed to start settlements and he would also have to send soldiers to protect the settlements. **Franciscan** padres would be needed in the new settlements to make friends with the Indians. The Franciscan padres would also be needed to start missions along the Alta California coast.

RESPONSIBLE LEADERS ARE CHOSEN

Gálvez knew that he needed brave, **responsible** leaders for the long journey to Alta California. He asked Gaspár de Portolá to be the commander-in-chief of the expeditions. Portolá was a brave soldier and the governor of **Baja California**. Portolá promised to take soldiers and supplies to Alta California. Gálvez was pleased that Portolá would be on the expedition because Portolá was reliable and well-liked by his men.

Father Junípero Serra, the president of the missions in Baja California, was also asked by Gálvez to go on the expeditions to Alta California. Father Serra was needed to teach the Indians and start a chain of missions along the California coast.

There are towns and buildings in California today named after Portolá, a brave man and a strong leader. He became a soldier in Spain at age eleven!

PREPARATIONS ARE MADE

Gálvez, Portolá and Father Serra agreed that there were to be both sea and land expeditions traveling from Baja California to Alta California. The sea expeditions were to have three ships, the *San Carlos*, the *San José*, and the *San Antonio*, to carry supplies to the harbors of San Diego and Monterey. The land expeditions would march overland to San Diego Bay and meet two of the ships while the third ship sailed on to Monterey Bay.

Many supplies were gathered for these journeys. Cloth, beads, and dried fruit and meat were packed as gifts for the Indians. Captain Gálvez made sure that the ships were loaded with smoked meats, cheese, wine, corn, biscuits, flour, rice, and chocolate as well as tools and equipment for starting the new missions. Although the Baja California missions were very poor, they gave seeds, tools, animals, candlesticks, church bells, and **vestments** for the new missions in Alta California.

Some of the foods that the sailors ate on the long sea voyage to Alta California included cheese, hard biscuits, dried fruit, beef jerky, and beans.

Supply List for the San Carlos
Captain, Vicente Vila

Provisions for sea voyage and mission supplies

4,676 lbs meat	1275 lbs brown sugar
1,783 lbs fish	125 lbs sugar
10 hams	275 lbs chocolate
6 live cattle	11 bottles oil
230 bushels maize	17 bushels salt
575 lbs lentils	2 lbs spice
945 lbs chickpeas	125 lbs garlic
495 lbs beans	300 lbs red pepper
1300 lbs flour	6 crates figs
15 sacks bran	3 crates raisins
945 lbs rice	2 crates dates
6,678 lbs common bread	5 jars brandy
690 lbs white bread	6 jars wine
3,800 gallons water	112 lbs candles
450 lbs cheese	5 tons wood
500 lbs lard	16 sacks coal
7 jars vinegar	$1,000 in coins

January 5, 1769

Vicente Vila

These are some of the supplies that were gathered and loaded aboard the ships that would go to Alta California. Can you identify some of these supplies? What other supplies would have been taken on this journey?

The decision had been made! The leaders were chosen! Preparations had been completed! The sea and land expeditions were ready to journey to Alta California. Captain Portolá and the soldiers were going north to Alta California to secure land for Spain, chart harbors for the Manila Galleons, and map out lands for Spanish towns and forts. Father Serra and the padres would start missions and teach the Indians the Christian religion. These explorations and colonizations would keep other countries such as Russia and England from taking the Spanish territory of Alta California.

Now, you have met the brave explorers Columbus, Magellan, Drake, Cabrillo, Vizcaíno, Portolá, and Father Serra, who like many brave men and women today have journeyed into unexplored worlds.

This is the Spanish banner that was probably carried by Portolá in 1769 on the expedition into Alta California.

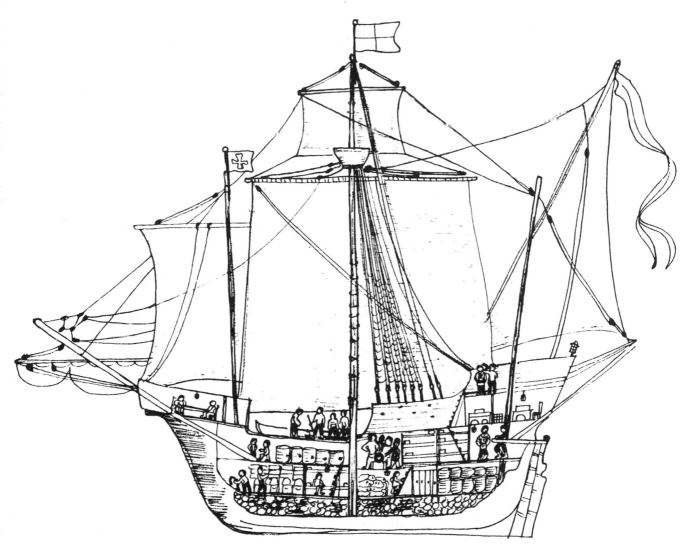

Look carefully at this cutaway picture of a caravel. Can you find the following areas on this ship? The bottom of the ship was filled with stone or ballast so the ship would not tip over. Supplies, food, and water were kept on the lowest deck. The crew's cabin was on the same deck as the supplies. The officers' cabin and the steersman's cabin were on the deck above the supplies. The rowboat and the outdoor cooking area were on the main deck. The captain's cabin was on the very top deck.

Before the voyage, the bottoms of the ships were smeared with tallow and pitch, and sand and stones were put into the holds of the ships for ballast. Firewood for cooking was brought on board and lashed down. Meals were usually cooked over a small open fire built in a box of sand. Biscuits, beans, salted meats, and other foods that wouldn't spoil were brought on board.

FATHER JUNÍPERO SERRA

Today, I, Junípero Serra founded the ninth mission along the El Camino Reál in Alta California. My dream of bringing the message of God's love to the Indians has come true.

I was born on November 24, 1713 on the island of **Majorca** near the coast of Spain. I went to classes at a school where the teachers belonged to the **Order of Saint Francis**. My teachers often spoke of the New World. When I became a padre, I knew I wanted to be a missionary in this new land.

Finally, I made the decision to become a missionary and travel to the New World. The idea of traveling alone to the New World worried me. One evening, an old friend, Father Francisco Palóu, told me that he too was going on a missionary journey to the New World. I was happy that I wouldn't be going on the long journey by myself.

Father Palóu and I joined nineteen other missionaries and left Spain in August of 1749. It took the captain of our ship and his crew 99 days to sail across the Atlantic Ocean to New Spain. Our ocean voyage was rough and difficult. We finally docked in the seaport of Vera Cruz and then started a 300-mile journey across the coastal plains and high mountains to Mexico City.

After many days of walking, one of my legs became swollen, blistered, and badly infected, but I continued the journey without resting because I knew how much I was needed at the college in Mexico City. On the very last day of the year 1749, we finally arrived in Mexico City.

I lived and studied in Mexico City for five months and then I **volunteered** to work with the Indians in the Sierra Gorda Mountains. Five missions had already been started in these mountains, but the padres there found it difficult to live in the hot climate. They were often ill and never stayed long enough to learn the language of the Indians. It was difficult to grow food in these mountains and much of the food had to come on mule back from Mexico City.

I spent nine years with the Indians of the Sierra Gorda Mountains in New Spain. I worked in the fields with the Indians and showed them how to plant and grow their own food. In the evenings, I spent many hours learning the language so that I could speak with the Indians and teach them about God.

I returned to Mexico City in 1758 where I worked for nine more years as a **home missionary**. Some of my duties were choir director, teaching new padres, and preaching.

In 1767, I was sent to Baja California as the President of the Baja California missions. Father Palóu and Father Crespí were also assigned to these missions. I remember how I walked across the rocky lands to visit each of these missions.

I had just begun my work in Baja California, when, in 1769, Viceroy Galvéz asked me to join Gaspár de Portolá on an expedition to Alta California. I was needed to teach the Indians and start a chain of missions on the Alta California coast. What a happy day this was for me! My dream was about to come true!

I'll never forget how excited everyone was when my expedition left La Paz in New Spain and began the long journey north to San Diego. It was a hard journey, but when we reached the beautiful bay of San Diego, I knew in my heart that this would be the beginning of a great plan to settle this land.

Although we had many problems starting the mission in San Diego, we succeeded and I was soon blessing the site for a second mission on the shores of Monterey Bay. I founded seven more missions and it will soon be time for other padres to continue my work along the *El Camino Reál.*

Today, I am tired and I have difficulty breathing. My feet and legs are swollen. I feel my life will soon be over. I have lived seventy years, nine months, and four days, having been a padre for one half of my life and in Alta California for sixteen years. I leave behind me four presidios, two planned pueblos, and nine missions. I know there will soon be more missions along the *El Camino Reál* and my spirit shall always be with them!

Retrato del Rev. Padre Fray Junípero Serra Aposto de la Alta California, tomado del original que se conserva en su Convento de la Santa Cruz de Querétaro.

In 1692, seventy-seven years before Father Serra started the first mission in Alta California, Father Eusebio Kino was sent into what is now the southern part of Arizona. Father Kino was a Jesuit missionary and spent over thirty years in the Southwest. He was also an explorer, cartographer, astronomer, builder, historian, and agriculturist. Father Kino founded a chain of twenty-four missions and nineteen ranchos and made fourteen expeditions into the land that is now Arizona.

BACKTRACKING

1. José de Gálvez was the King of Spain's special representative in New Spain. Name three things that he did for the king.

2. Gálvez made plans to send an expedition to Alta California. Who were the leaders that Gálvez decided to send to Alta California?

3. What were the responsibilities of the two leaders on this expedition to Alta California?

4. Many supplies were gathered for the expedition to Alta California. Name five things that were to be taken to Alta California.

BRAVE EXPLORERS

1. Look carefully at the supply list for the ship, the *San Carlos*, in this chapter. What is missing from this supply list that would have kept many sailors from dying of scurvy?

Mark Leibowitz and his sister, Susan, are about to explore Father Kino's mission, San Xavier in Arizona.

When the ship the *San Carlos* left La Paz, there was a great celebration. The anchor was pulled up and the *San Carlos* sailed out of the harbor of La Paz on January 9, 1769. Captain Vila had orders to sail to San Diego.

CHAPTER SIX

ALTA CALIFORNIA BY LAND AND BY SEA

SEA EXPEDITIONS

The expeditions to Alta California began on January 9, 1769 when the ship, the *San Carlos*, left La Paz in New Spain. Aboard the *San Carlos* were Captain Vila and twenty-three sailors, Doctor Pedro Prat, Padre Parron, two blacksmiths, four cooks, an engineer, a **cosmographer**, and Lieutenant Fages with 25 soldiers. Lieutenant Fages kept a diary of this sea journey. There were sixty-two persons in all aboard the *San Carlos*.

More than a month later another ship, the *San Antonio*, sailed from La Paz. It arrived in San Diego harbor about two months later and *before* the ship, the *San Carlos*! When the *San Carlos* finally arrived in San Diego for the **rendevous** with the *San Antonio*, many men on the *San Carlos* had died of scurvy and had been buried at sea. The remaining men on board the *San Carlos* were so sick with scurvy that they did not have the strength to leave the ship. Captain Pérez and his men from the *San Antonio* had to go to the *San Carlos* to help the sick men off the ship.

Lieutenant Fages sailed aboard the *San Carlos* to Alta California. He kept a diary of the sea journey. During his lifetime, he kept diaries of all his travels in Alta California. He became the governor of Alta California two different times.

LAND EXPEDITIONS

In March, 1769, the first land expedition started out to **blaze** a trail over the rugged countryside to San Diego. Father Crespi, a good friend of Father Serra, and a man named Captain Rivera were in this first land expedition along with twenty-five leather-jacketed soldiers and forty-two Baja California Indians. Their purpose was to find a good trail so that future expeditions would have a route to follow. They took with them 200 cattle and more than 200 horses and mules. The mules carried food, tools, and seeds for the settlements that were going to be started in Alta California. It was a very difficult trip going to San Diego. The land was rugged and caring for the animals was a hard job. Can you imagine taking a journey with over 400 bawling, braying, mooing animals? What would it be like to herd these hungry creatures through dry, dusty valleys and steep, rocky ravines? How would you feed and water so many animals? What a long, slow trip it would be traveling through rugged lands to an unfamiliar destination! It took this first land expedition 60 days to reach San Diego.

In May, the second land expedition started traveling north to San Diego Bay. Gaspár de Portolá and Father Serra were with the group. The men and animals followed the trail made by the first land expedition. The great **caravan** was a long noisy group of men and pack animals as it moved along through the steep passes and rough, rocky hills. This second land expedition was grateful to the men who had traveled

this way several weeks earlier. The first land expedition had marked the trail to show the location of fresh
water, green grass for the animals, and good
campsites.

Leather-jacket soldiers (soldados de cuera) came to Alta California with the first
land expedition. Their leader was Captain Rivera. They came from a presidio in
Loreto, New Spain. Each soldier wore a cuera (vest or sleeveless jacket) made
of seven or eight layers of sheep or deer skin. The cuera was protection against
Indian arrows. Each soldier wore a shoulder belt that held bullets and gunpow-
der for his guns. Besides pistols and guns, each man carried a sword, shield,
and a lance. One soldier was given extra pay to take care of his company's
equipment and see that all the equipment was oiled and cleaned. Each soldier
was also given six horses, a colt, and a mule. All of this equipment plus the soldiers' wages must have cost the King of Spain a lot of money!

   The soldiers had to be between 18 and 30 years of age and at least two varas
in height (one vara is equal to 33 inches). These soldiers were brave, responsible, and trustworthy men. Some of the soldiers who later came to Alta California
were not as responsible or honest as these first leather-jacket soldiers.

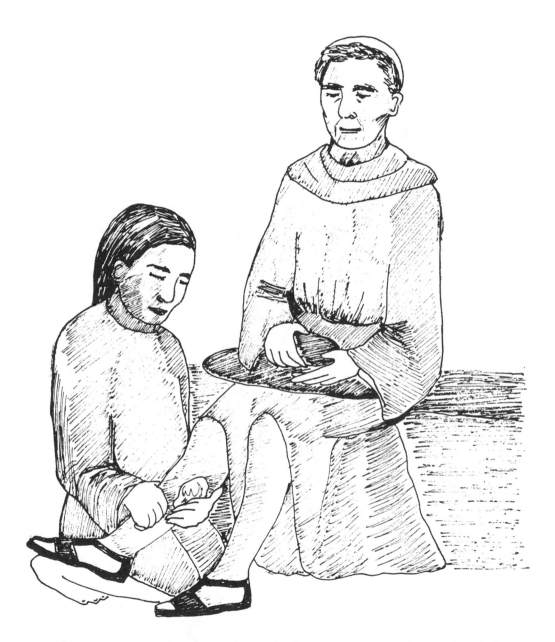

Although the journey for the second land party was somewhat easier, Father Serra suffered greatly because of an old sore on his leg. This sore became more and more painful. Finally, one of the mule drivers gave Father Serra a medicine made of tallow and herbs to rub on his sore leg. Father Serra was soon well enough to complete the journey to San Diego.

THE RENDEZVOUS AT SAN DIEGO

In July, 1769, the second land party reached San Diego. At last, all four groups of the great expedition that had been planned by Gálvez, Portolá, and Father Serra were together in San Diego. Everyone had suffered many hardships on the long, dangerous journey to Alta California. Almost one half of all the people who had come to San Diego had become ill and died. Their food was almost gone and many people wanted to return to New Spain. Father Serra and Captain Portolá refused to give up because they knew it was important to start missions and **presidios** in San Diego and Monterey as soon as possible.

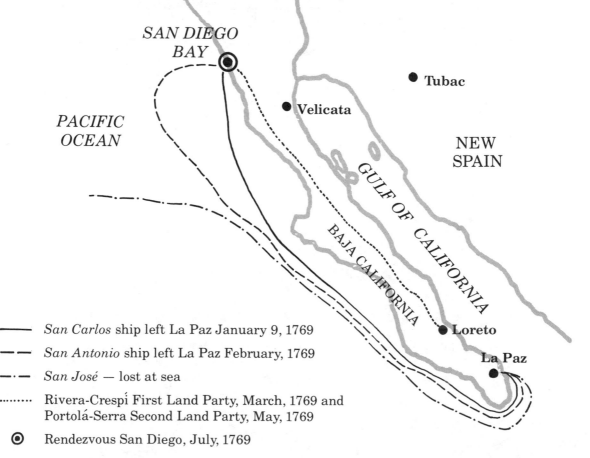

————— *San Carlos* ship left La Paz January 9, 1769

– – – *San Antonio* ship left La Paz February, 1769

–·–·– *San José* — lost at sea

········· Rivera-Crespí First Land Party, March, 1769 and Portolá-Serra Second Land Party, May, 1769

◉ Rendezvous San Diego, July, 1769

THE FIRST LINK IN THE MISSION CHAIN

On July 16, 1769, Father Serra **blessed** the first mission buildings at San Diego. They were simple shelters of brush and branches. Grasses and tules were used for roofs. A large wooden cross was placed near a **chapel** made of brush and reeds. Captain Portolá and his soldiers started a presidio where the soldiers could live.

The mission got off to a slow start. Even though the Indians were curious, they did not trust the Spanish newcomers and would not accept food from the padres. The Indians were fascinated with woven material, but even gifts of cloth could not make the Indians stay at the mission. Father Serra hoped that some of the Indians would come to be **baptized**, but the few Indians who visited the mission were frightened by the soldiers and would not stay.

Father Serra never gave up hope of bringing more and more Indians to the mission. He prayed that Indians would come to the first mission in Alta California, San Diego de Alcalá.

The first shelters at San Diego were built by the padres and the soldiers.

San Diego de Alcalá was the first mission in Alta California founded by Father Serra in 1769. In 1774, Father Serra decided to rebuild the mission six miles away. Father Serra felt that the Indians were happier away from the soldiers. Also, more land was needed for crops. This picture shows Mission San Diego in 1937.

About seven years after Mission San Diego had been built, a large group of Indians attacked the mission, burned the buildings, and killed three people at the mission. Today, there is a large white cross at the mission marking the place where one of the padres, Father Jayme, died during the Indian attack.

Campanarios were built at many of the missions. A campanario is a wall with openings in it where bells could be hung.

Mission San Diego has a beautiful campanario or bell tower. This bell tower was rebuilt about fifty years ago.

MEET PEDRO PRAT

Everyone in New Spain was talking about the land and sea expeditions that were going to Alta California to start Spanish settlements. I wanted to take part in this great adventure, so I, Pedro Prat, signed on board the ship, *San Carlos*, as the ship's doctor. As a doctor, my job is helping the sick. I clean wounds or **cauterize** open cuts, but my duty on board the *San Carlos* was to shave the ship's officers each day!

After many weeks at sea nearly all of the sailors, soldiers, and mechanics on board the *San Carlos* became ill with scurvy. These men could not walk or eat. I spent most of my time giving water to men who were too sick to get out of their bunks. No one knew what caused scurvy and there was no help for these sick and dying men.

When we finally anchored at San Diego Bay, the sick men had to be carried ashore and placed on tule mats to rest. When the land expeditions arrived, I helped Captain Portolá and Father Serra set up shelters for these sick men. After a few weeks, Portolá and several men left to look for Monterey Bay. Father Serra and I were left at San Diego to care for more than fifty sick men.

When Captain Portolá returned to San Diego, many of the men on his expedition were still so sick with scurvy that they had to be carried. Nearly half of all the men who had come to Alta California on the sea and land expeditions from New Spain died of scurvy or **dehydration**.

I had come on this expedition from New Spain to help others and I was not able to help those who needed me the most!

BACKTRACKING

1. A cartographer draws maps. A cosmographer describes the land. Why are both of these persons important to an expedition?

2. Why was it important that the Spanish start missions in San Diego and Monterey as soon as possible?

3. Where was the first mission in Alta California built? What was the date?

4. Why didn't the Indians in San Diego want to stay at the mission?

5. Why were presidios built near the missions in Alta California?

BRAVE EXPLORERS

1. How do you think the first land party marked the trail for the second land party traveling into Alta California? Would they have used stones, flags, sticks, notes, etc.?

Mission San Diego today

Portolá discovered one of the greatest harbors in the world, San Francisco Bay!

CHAPTER SEVEN
A PRAYER IS ANSWERED

PORTOLÁ JOURNEYS NORTH

While Father Serra was busy with the mission at San Diego, Portolá sent the ship, the *San Antonio*, and eight sailors back to New Spain for fresh supplies. These sailors were still sick with scurvy. Portolá then headed north to find Monterey Bay with Captain Rivera and Lieutenant Fages, thirty-five soldiers, a mapmaker, two padres, and fifteen Baja California mission Indians. This journey was a difficult one. Although the beautiful land of California was filled with deer, elk, flocks of ducks and geese, seeds, grains, berries, and nuts, the Spanish explorers grew weaker each day from scurvy and lack of supplies. Do you think they were too weak and ill from scurvy to hunt for rabbits and deer? Hunting wild **game** needs skill and accuracy. If you are ill, it would be hard work to track and kill a rabbit or deer.

Portolá finally reached Monterey Bay, but did not recognize the bay from the maps he was using. Here he expected to meet the ship, *San José*, the third ship in the expedition to leave New Spain. Unfortunately, this supply ship never reached land after leaving La Paz. All on board the *San José* were drowned at sea. Portolá, not knowing of this tragedy, continued to travel north looking for Monterey Bay and the supply ship, *San José*. He went on to discover one of the greatest harbors in the world, San Francisco Bay.

RETURN TO SAN DIEGO

Portolá's men were now so weak and tired that he was forced to return to the mission at San Diego. Many of the explorers were so sick that they had to be carried on **litters**. The starving men had to shoot and eat their faithful mules because they did not have the strength to hunt game from the land.

When Portolá finally returned to San Diego, after having been gone six months, he found many problems. The ship, *San Antonio*, that he had sent back to New Spain for fresh supplies, had not yet arrived in San Diego. Many men in Portolá's expedition as well as those at San Diego were ill and wanted to go home to New Spain. Many men had died. The Indians were not friendly. How could these sick and starving Spanish people settle a new land for the King of Spain?

A PRAYER IS ANSWERED

At last Gaspár de Portolá decided that everyone in the expedition would return to New Spain. Father Serra begged him to wait nine more days for the return of the supply ship, the *San Antonio*. Portolá agreed to wait, but he was sure the supply ship would not return to San Diego. For nine days the padres prayed for the return of the ship. Father Serra believed in his heart that their prayers would be answered.

On the afternoon of the ninth day, Father Serra climbed a small hill as he had done so many times before to watch for the ship, the *San Antonio*. An incredible thing happened! The white **billowing** sails of the *San Antonio* appeared on the **horizon**. Father Serra's prayers had been answered! The supply ship had returned! The first Spanish settlement at San Diego had been saved!

On Portolá's return from San Francisco Bay, many of his men were so weak and sick that they had to be carried on litters.

THE SECOND JOURNEY TO MONTEREY

Six months after the founding of the new mission in San Diego, Portolá planned to journey northward again in search of Monterey Bay. Captain Portolá, Father Crespi, soldiers, and Baja California Indians started on the trail north to Monterey. Twelve soldiers were taken on this journey and eight were left to help at San Diego. Perhaps, this time the journey did not seem so far because Portolá and Crespi knew the way.

Five weeks later, Captain Portolá and Father Crespi stood on a low hill overlooking a beautiful bay. There was no doubt now in Portolá's mind that he had found Monterey Bay. This was the beautiful bay that had been named Monterey Bay in the year 1602 by Captain Sebastián Vizcaino.

After a sea journey of six weeks from San Diego, the ship, *San Antonio*, anchored in Monterey Bay. Aboard the ship were more soldiers and supplies. Father Serra, the President of the Alta California missions, was also aboard. Father Serra had wanted to come to Monterey with Portolá's land expedition, but Portolá had insisted that Father Serra go by ship. Why do you think Captain Portolá insisted that Father Serra go by ship instead of marching with the soldiers from San Diego to Monterey?

THE SECOND LINK IN THE MISSION CHAIN

With great joy, Father Serra came ashore at Monterey and asked for God's blessing on this land. He then founded the site for the second mission in California. Everyone set to work building shelters out of branches. An **altar** was built under a huge oak tree near the beach and bells were hung from a strong limb of the tree. On June 3, 1770, Father Serra founded Mission San Carlos Borromeo de Carmelo and Captain Portolá founded the site for the new presidio where Spanish soldiers would live.

The founding ceremonies for Mission San Carlos Borromeo and the presidio were very special. When news of this great celebration reached Mexico City, every church bell was rung to honor the founding of Mission San Carlos Borromeo.

The presidios were built to protect the mission padres. The presidios were built near the coast and a ditch 12 to 16 feet wide and 6 to 8 feet deep was dug around them for protection. Inside the presidio was a large open area surrounded by high walls. Soldiers and visitors went in and out through a main gate which was guarded by soldiers. Guards were also on duty at all times in the four watch towers on the four corners of the presidio.

Father Serra's room at Mission San Carlos Borromeo was small and bare.

Now that the missions and presidios at San Diego and Monterey had been founded, Portolá turned his command over to young Lieutenant Pedro Fages who took over Portolá's duties as military commander. Lieutenant Fages now became the governor of Alta California. Portolá sailed back to New Spain on the ship, the *San Antonio*.

Father Serra, the soldiers, and the Baja California Indians started building brush shelters, **barracks**, warehouses, and a **stockade** or pole fence to enclose these buildings. One of the smaller buildings was used as a mission chapel. There was not enough good soil to plant mission gardens and the land was hard to **irrigate**. The Indians accepted gifts from the padres, but the Indians were afraid of the soldiers. Because of these problems, Father Serra decided to move the location of Mission San Carlos Borromeo to a new place in the Carmel Valley where the land was **fertile** and the Carmel River ran nearby. The new location of the mission would still be close enough to the Monterey Presidio for protection.

Father Serra lived in a small hut beside the church of Mission San Carlos Borromeo and greeted all visitors in this **humble** home. Father Serra loved Mission San Carlos Borromeo so much that he made this mission the capital of all the California missions. For fifty years, many of the mission presidents that followed Father Serra made Mission San Carlos Borromeo their headquarters.

The first church of Mission San Carlos Borromeo was built of logs and has been rebuilt six times. This is how the mission church looked before 1884. A visitor in 1861 reported that squirrels scampered through holes in the mission walls, cattle roamed through the mission rooms, and birds nested in the alcoves.

BACKTRACKING

1. Who discovered San Francisco Bay?

2. Give three reasons why the men wanted to leave San Diego and return to New Spain.

3. Why do you think Father Serra traveled to Monterey aboard ship?

4. Portolá's second journey to Monterey was easier than his first journey. Why do you think this was so?

5. Why do you think stockades were built around mission buildings?

6. Give three reasons why Father Serra changed the location of Mission San Carlos Borromeo.

BRAVE EXPLORERS

1. Pretend you are in charge of feeding fifty-five hungry explorers on an expedition to Alta California. Supplies are running low. Tell three things that you would do to get food for your group.

2. Why do you think Father Serra made Mission San Carlos Borromeo his headquarters? What would be special about the land around this mission that would please Father Serra?

El Camino Reál, The King's Highway, is the road that connected all of the California missions and later served as one of California's major stagecoach and wagon roads. It was named and used by the mission padres. The Spanish people hoped that one day the King of Spain would visit Alta California and travel this road named in his honor. Long ago it took about a day to go from one mission to the next. Now it may take less than an hour! Today, our modern Highway 101 still follows parts of the *El Camino Reál.* If you look carefully at this picture, you can see the original *El Camino Reál* as it passes this mission. Think of how many padres, soldiers, and settlers walked along this famous road!

76

CHAPTER EIGHT

NEW MISSIONS AND NEW SETTLERS

MORE PADRES ARRIVE

In the spring of 1771, ten padres arrived in Alta California and Father Serra began to make plans for the founding of more missions up and down the coast of Alta California. He wanted these missions to be a day's journey apart so that travelers would not have to set up camp on the open road. The Spanish named the road that would connect all the missions the *El Camino Reál*. *El Camino Reál* means the King's Highway. The *El Camino Reál* followed some seven hundred miles of California's length.

THE THIRD LINK IN THE MISSION CHAIN

Father Serra left the Carmel mission to establish the third mission in the Valley of the Oaks near today's King City. This new mission was called San Antonio de Padua. At the site where the mission was to be built, Father Serra hung a bell on the limb of a tree. He rang the bell loudly and one Indian came to watch. Father Serra gave the Indian gifts of colored beads and fruit and showed such kindness that the Indian left to return with other members of his tribe. The Indians brought gifts of acorns, pine nuts, and seeds that they had gathered. As time went by, the Indians helped build a church, barracks, and a house for the padres. Because of the Indian help, San Antonio de Padua eventually had many buildings, great numbers of livestock, and fine orchards of fruits and olives. Mission San Antonio de Padua went on to become one of the finest and largest missions in California.

When Mission San Antonio de Padua was started, the Indians were very helpful. These friendly Indians were good craftsmen and helped to build the mission shelters. They also helped to plant crops and care for the livestock. When more help was needed, Indians from Mission San Carlos Borromeo were sent to help. This picture shows Mission San Antonio de Padua as it looks today.

THE FOURTH LINK IN THE MISSION CHAIN

San Gabriel Arcángel was the fourth in Father Junípero Serra's chain of Alta California missions. Father Serra had selected this site in the summer of 1771. He sent Padre Cambón and Padre Somera with a guard of ten soldiers and a supply train of mules to start the fourth mission. The two padres raised a cross and started the fourth mission, San Gabriel Arcángel, on September 8, 1771.

Mission San Gabriel was started in 1771. Ten years later a party of settlers founded the little town of Los Angeles nearby. The outside of this mission is very beautiful. Look carefully at this picture of the mission today and you will see (far right) the famous outside stairs leading to the choir loft.

The grey robed padres at Mission San Gabriel worked with the Indians, but the soldiers were especially **crude** and **boisterous**. The soldiers did not get along with the padres and caused many problems with the Indians. The soldiers refused to work, paid no attention to their commanding officer, frightened and chased Indians to their homes, and terrified Indian women and children. The Indians were helpless against the soldiers' guns and horses and because of the problems caused by the soldiers, many Indians would not come to Mission San Gabriel. It took many years before the Indians came to the mission and learned to trust the padres.

THE FIFTH LINK IN THE MISSION CHAIN

Father Serra received news that two ships loaded with supplies were anchored in San Diego and would not sail any farther north because of strong winds. Father Serra needed supplies for the missions and he decided he must go to San Diego to persuade the ships' captains to sail north to Monterey. Governor Fages went along with Father Serra to meet the two ships at San Diego.

Father Serra decided that on this journey to San Diego he would start the fifth mission near the Valley of the Bears where earlier that year Governor Fages had hunted bears and had given bear meat to the Indians. In September, 1772, Father Serra raised a cross and he founded the fifth mission which he named San Luis Obispo de Tolosa. Fages and Father Serra went on to San Diego and left Father José Cavaller to begin building the mission. Father Serra left flour, chocolate, and brown sugar to trade with the Indians. Father Serra also left seeds for Father Cavaller to plant and start the first crops at the mission.

Work started at once at Mission San Luis Obispo. The five soldiers who were left to help Father Cavaller started building their barracks and a stockade. Father Cavaller and two Indian **neophytes** from Baja California started building tule huts and a chapel of logs. The Indians at San Luis Obispo were friendly because they remembered how Fages had rid their valley of troublesome bears and given them bear meat a few years before. The Indians helped the padres and soldiers build the mission and the Indians often brought fresh **venison** to trade for beads, brown sugar, or chocolate.

Mission San Luis Obispo had a good start. Indians from Baja California were sent to the mission to teach the Alta California Indians how to weave, cultivate the fields, and care for the livestock. This picture shows Mission San Luis Obispo almost one hundred years after it had been started by Father Serra.

GOVERNOR FAGES AND FATHER SERRA

When Governor Fages and Father Serra arrived in San Diego, they made sure that fresh supplies were sent north to the missions. Father Serra then asked Governor Fages to help him start another mission, but the governor refused because there were not enough soldiers to protect a sixth mission. After several arguments with Fages, Father Serra decided to go to Mexico City and ask the viceroy for help. Father Serra wanted supplies to be sent regularly to the new missions. He wanted more soldiers to guard the missions and he wanted the soldiers to be able to bring their families to Alta California. Father Serra also wanted the viceroy to replace Governor Fages with a new governor for Alta California.

FATHER SERRA ARRIVES IN MEXICO CITY

In 1772, Father Serra arrived in Mexico City and told the viceroy of his plans for Alta California. The viceroy liked Father Serra's plans and ordered supply ships to go regularly to Alta California and carry fresh supplies all the way to Monterey. The viceroy also named Captain Rivera as the new governor of Alta California. You probably remember that Captain Rivera led the first land party to San Diego in 1769. He was the captain of the leather-jacket soldiers.

The viceroy thought about what Father Serra had said about bringing soldiers and their families to the new missions in Alta California. For many years the Spanish had traveled to Alta California by the rough trail from Baja California and by the slow and dangerous sea route. Now, the viceroy felt that a new, easier, and safer way to bring families to Alta California was needed. Who would help bring families to the new missions in Alta California? What routes would they use?

In 1772, Governor Fages traveled to San Diego with Father Serra. When Father Serra went on to Mexico City, Fages returned north and according to maps, possibly passed this rock formation. The authors feel that Fages or one of his men may have inscribed "Espana Escudo" (I have left Spain) on one of the rocks.

JUAN BAUTISTA DE ANZA, PATHFINDER

Juan Bautista de Anza, an explorer, was asked by the viceroy to find safe trails from New Spain to Alta California for the Spanish families. Anza explored the deserts and the mountains of southeastern California. In 1774, Anza, his men, Father Garcés, and Father Díaz left Sonora in New Spain and traveled westward. They crossed the deserts and mountains and after a difficult journey, came to Mission San Gabriel. The padres and people at the mission were very surprised to see the explorers. Now, Anza knew that he could take families to Alta California using this new route through the deserts and mountains.

Anza's second expedition to Alta California began in 1775 from Sonora in New Spain. Two hundred forty people, mostly soldiers and their families came with Anza. Father Garcés also traveled with this expedition. During the six month journey from Sonora to California, the number of colonists grew due to the birth of several babies.

Great was the joy of Juan Bautista de Anza and the colonists when they reached Mission San Gabriel. Here they rested and then went on to the mission in Monterey where most of the colonists stayed. Now, there were two land trails to California. One trail came up the coast from Baja California and the other trail led from Sonora over the deserts and mountains to the broad **plain** where Mission San Gabriel had been built.

Anza was a great leader and explorer.

JUAN BAUTISTA DE ANZA'S ROUTE
FROM TUBAC TO MISSION SAN GABRIEL

Anza, his men, and over 200 colonists left Tubac in Sonora, New Spain. They traveled northwest through the Great Desert in Sonora and crossed the Colorado River near the Yuma Indian villages. After traveling through more desert, Anza's party passed the Cahuilla Indian villages at the foot of the mountains and continued on to the Santa Ana River. After splashing across the Santa Ana River, it was a short journey to Mission San Gabriel.

THE SIXTH LINK IN THE MISSION CHAIN

In the spring of 1776, Anza, a few soldiers, Father Pedro Font, and Lieutenant Moraga left Monterey and journeyed to San Francisco Bay. Anza chose a site for the third presidio and three miles away he marked the site of the sixth mission, San Francisco de Asís. Anza returned to Monterey, told the colonists good-bye, and journeyed back to Sonora in New Spain. Anza left Lieutenant Moraga in charge of bringing colonists to start a presidio and a mission in San Francisco. Lieutenant Moraga and Father Palóu, Father Serra's good friend, journeyed to San Francisco and started the new mission settlement on June 29, 1776 just five days before the signing of the Declaration of Independence in Philadelphia, Pennsylvania.

In October of 1776, when the mission buildings were almost finished, a great celebration was held. There was a parade as well as fireworks, firing of cannons, chanting, and singing. Mission San Francisco de Asis was frequently called Mission Dolores.

Mission San Francisco de Asís in the year 1856

These Alta California Indians are performing ceremonial dances in front of Mission San Francisco de Asís.

Soon after the first mission buildings of San Francisco de Asís were started, the ship *San Carlos*, sailed into the bay to bring supplies to the presidio and mission. It was the first ship to sail into San Francisco Bay. The ship's carpenters helped build the heavy carved front doors of the mission.

San Francisco de Asís, 1986

THE SEVENTH AND EIGHTH LINKS IN THE MISSION CHAIN

The seventh link in the mission chain, Mission San Juan Capistrano, was founded twice. In 1775, Father Lasuén was sent by Father Serra to begin this new mission. Father Lasuén had been at San Juan Capistrano for only one week when he heard about Indian problems at San Diego. Quickly he buried the founding bells. Father Lasuén and the few people who had helped him start the mission, hurried off to San Diego.

One year later, Father Serra journeyed to San Juan Capistrano. He dug up the bells, hung them from a tree and on November 1, 1776, Father Serra founded the mission a second time.

The Indians were friendly and helped with the building of this mission. The climate was good and the crops grew well. Mission San Juan Capistrano was one of the most successful missions in the Alta California mission chain.

VIEW OF THE RUINS OF THE CHURCH, AND BUILDINGS OF THE EX-MISSION OF SAN JUAN CAPISTRANO. THE CHURCH DESTROYED BY THE EARTHQUAKE OF 1812

Mission San Juan Capistrano is known as "The Jewel of the Missions". At one time it had seven great domes. In 1812, an earthquake destroyed most of this beautiful church. This picture was painted in 1865.

Mission Santa Clara de Asís, the eighth mission, was founded in January of 1777. The site for this mission had been selected by Juan Bautista de Anza a year before and was located beside the Guadalupe River at the southern end of San Francisco Bay. Lieutenant Moraga, some soldiers, and their families started the first church and planned the other buildings. They waited for Father José Murguía who was to travel from Monterey with church supplies, livestock, and tools. When Father Murguía arrived, everyone worked together to start the new mission buildings.

In the following years, the church had to be moved many times due to floods. The third and last church at Mission Santa Clara that Father Murguía designed and helped to build was one of the most beautiful churches in California. Father Murguía died the day after this church was finished. He was well-liked and had baptized almost 700 Indians during the seven years that he served at Mission Santa Clara de Asís.

This is the first photograph taken of Mission Santa Clara de Asís. The year is 1853.

MISSION SAN BUENAVENTURA, THE NINTH LINK

Five years after the building of Mission Santa Clara, Mission San Buenaventura now standing in the city of Ventura in Southern California, was founded. This mission had originally been planned by Father Serra as the third mission to be started along the *El Camino Reál*. The original founding was put off for twelve years because of troubles at other missions. The other missions needed many guards and there were not enough guards to start Mission San Buenaventura. At last, in March of 1782, Father Serra and several soldiers with their families selected a site for the ninth mission. On Easter Sunday, 1782, Father Serra and Father Cambón said mass and officially founded Mission San Buenaventura.

These vaqueros are coming to Mission San Buenaventura. They have traveled along the *El Camino Reál* from Mission San Gabriel.

Over a century ago, at Mission San Buenaventura, this wooden bell was carved out of a block of wood. The wooden bell was used during special ceremonies when metal bells were not to be rung.

The Indians at Buenaventura were very friendly and helped with the building of the mission. The climate and the soil were excellent and crops grew well. The mission was successful for the first ten years and then several tragedies struck the mission. First, the church burned and had to be rebuilt. Three years later, the great earthquake of 1812 destroyed much of the mission. In 1818, the pirate Bouchard was rumored to be in the area. The mission padres quickly gathered all valuables such as paintings, statues, and silver. These were buried or hidden in caves. The padres then took the Indians, food, and livestock into the hills where they camped for over a month and waited for the pirate Bouchard to pass by. Soon after the padres and Indians had returned to the mission, the Mojave Indians came to trade. The soldiers would not allow the Mojave Indians to trade and locked them in the guardhouse. The next morning a furious fight started and some of the Mojave Indians were killed.

In later years, Mission San Buenaventura became known for its large crops of fruits and vegetables. Often sailing ships stopped at Mission San Buenaventura to get fresh supplies of food.

SANTA BARBARA PRESIDIO

After starting Mission San Buenaventura in 1782, Father Serra journeyed to Santa Barbara where he blessed the land and placed a cross on the site for the fourth presidio. Father Serra helped plan and start the military chapel at the presidio. Indians helped build this presidio. There was so much help given by the Indians that the men were able to construct buildings, an irrigation system, and start some farming.

Father Serra eagerly waited for the governor to give permission to start the tenth mission, Mission Santa Barbara. Governor Felipe de Neve had a new plan for the missions. He wanted this plan to be approved by the King of Spain before more missions were built in Alta California. This new plan greatly saddened Father Serra and he returned to Mission Carmel.

FATHER SERRA, FAITHFUL SERVANT OF GOD

In the spring of 1784, Father Serra decided to visit his nine missions. His diseased leg continued to cause him great pain and he was forced to return to Mission Carmel. His long, busy, helpful life was nearly over. He wrote farewell notes to the padres of the nine missions he had started and sent for his old friend, Father Palóu. When on August 28, 1784, he fell asleep to wake no more, the bells filled the air with music. From San Diego to San Francisco, the bells rang and rang to mark the passing of California's first great pioneer.

A cenotaph is a tomb or monument built in honor of a person whose body is buried elsewhere. This cenotaph at Mission San Carlos Borromeo is in honor of Father Serra. Father Serra's body is not in this cenotaph, but is buried near the altar of the church.

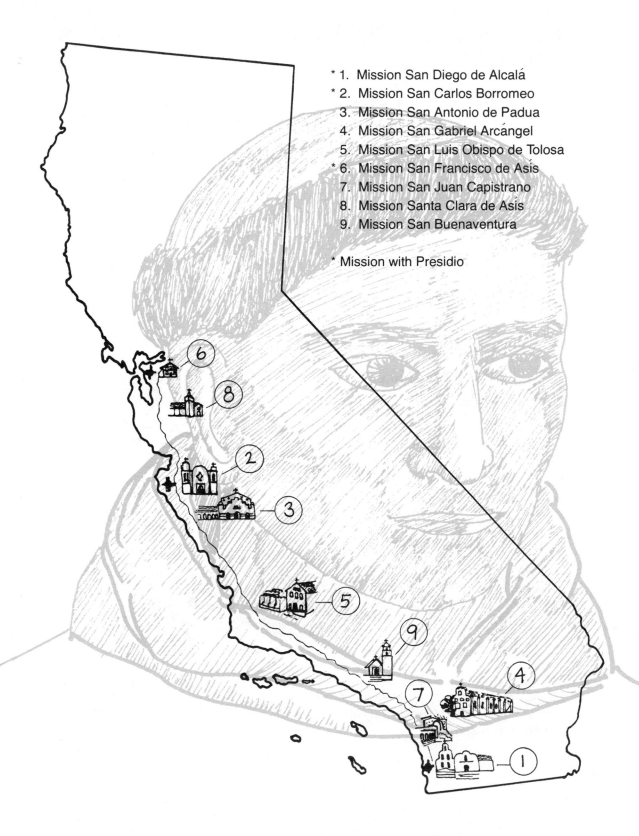

* 1. Mission San Diego de Alcalá
* 2. Mission San Carlos Borromeo
3. Mission San Antonio de Padua
4. Mission San Gabriel Arcángel
5. Mission San Luis Obispo de Tolosa
* 6. Mission San Francisco de Asís
7. Mission San Juan Capistrano
8. Mission Santa Clara de Asís
9. Mission San Buenaventura

* Mission with Presidio

BACKTRACKING

1. Why did Father Serra want the missions a day's journey apart?

2. Today, Highway 101 follows most of the *El Camino Reál*. Why do you think highway planners built a highway along this route?

3. Why did Father Serra want the viceroy to replace Governor Fages with a new governor?

4. Why was Juan Bautista de Anza important?

5. Who discovered San Francisco Bay before Anza established a mission there?

6. Pretend you are the Indian who watched Father Serra start Mission San Antonio de Padua. You are pleased that he has given you gifts of fruit and beads. When you return to your village what are you going to tell the people about the stranger you saw? How will you get the people to return with you to see the stranger?

7. Why didn't the Indians like the soldiers at Mission San Gabriel?

8. Why were the Indians at San Luis Obispo especially friendly to Father Serra and Governor Fages?

9. In late June, 1776, Mission San Francisco de Asís was founded. At this time, what historic event was taking place in Philadelphia, Pennsylvania?

10. Why did Mission San Juan Capistrano have to be founded twice?

11. Lieutenant Moraga was a very popular soldier. He helped the padres start several missions. When he helped start Mission Santa Clara, what do you think were his main duties?

12. The Mojave Indians often came to Mission San Buenaventura to trade. They came from the desert on the east side of the Tehachapi Mountains. What do you think they would bring to trade? What would they be trading for?

California Indians

CHAPTER NINE
MISSION LIFE

BUILDING A MISSION

THE PURPOSES OF THE ALTA CALIFORNIA MISSIONS

The Indians of California had lived in peace for thousands and thousands of years. Their lives were in **harmony** with nature as they lived in the beauty of the canyons, hills, and deserts. They knew that this land would be a part of them forever. As the centuries passed, Spanish people explored the land of California. Little did the Indians know that these first meetings with the Spanish would soon change their lives and their peaceful existence with nature.

As the first Spanish soldiers and Spanish padres arrived in California, the Indians' lives began to change. The padres came to show the Indians how to farm and how to live, eat, and dress like Europeans. The padres also came as missionaries to share their God with the Indians. What most of the padres did not realize was that the Indians already believed in God, but called him by a different name. For thousands of years, the Indians had lived in harmony with nature and knew that the Great Spirit was a part of them.

The Spanish soldiers came to Alta California to claim the land for Spain. As they marched through

Alta California, they claimed the valleys, rivers, mountains, and deserts for the King of Spain. The soldiers also came to protect the padres and make the Indians of California follow the rules of Spain.

PEOPLE WHO LIVED AND WORKED AT THE MISSIONS

At most missions there were two padres. It was necessary to have two padres at each mission to teach and supervise the many tasks that needed to be done. One padre was in charge of indoor activities while the other padre attended to outdoor activities. Each padre was able to do the duties of the other.

One padre kept a **journal** of the founding of the mission. He also kept a list of supplies that were used at the mission. This padre taught the Indians about the Christian God, led church services, performed baptisms, marriages, and other religious ceremonies. He kept a list of births, baptisms, marriages, and deaths.

The other padre at the mission was in charge of outdoor activities such as making adobe bricks and tiles, planting and harvesting crops, and taking care of the livestock.

The work of the Indian men at the missions was plowing, cultivating the soil, planting crops, making and laying adobe bricks, making limestone powder for plaster and for soaking corn and hides, tanning hides, making candles, threshing grain, tending cattle, horses, and sheep, and making shoes, **reatas**, and saddles from leather.

The work of the Indian women was **winnowing** the grain, spinning wool from the **fleece** of sheep, preparing corn and wheat for **tortillas** and bread, and preparing other foods. The Indian women also made baskets, washed clothing, and made soap.

The work of the Indian children was keeping animals out of the gardens, turning the adobe bricks that had been set out to dry, going to church school to learn the lessons of the church, scaring birds away from the grain fields, and helping their mothers with work.

The older Indians at the missions had the responsibility of teaching the younger Indians the customs and stories of their tribes. The older Indians also did their share of mission work such as sweeping, baking, weaving, weeding, and assisting the padres.

The California Indians worked hard building the California missions. They were taught how to do their jobs by the padres and by Indian workers who came from Baja California. The padres depended on the Indians to do all the work at the missions. Without the hardworking Indians, the missions could not have succeeded and Spain would not have been able to claim the land of Alta California!

The Alta California Indians painted colorful pictures on the inside walls of the mission churches. The Indians also painted religious pictures that were hung on the walls of the churches.

BUILDING MISSIONS IN ALTA CALIFORNIA

The padres selected **sites** for missions where there was a water supply for the mission, gardens, and crops. This meant finding a good stream or river. Good soil was needed to grow crops as well as a pleasant climate. The best sites were found near the coast or in the valleys.

Settlements of friendly Indians were necessary when selecting a site for a mission because the padres' plan was to teach the California Indians about God. The padres also needed these Indians to build missions and learn the jobs and duties at a mission.

EARLY MISSION SHELTERS

The first mission buildings were simple huts made of mud and sticks. The roofs were made with tules or reeds. A large wooden cross was always placed near the church and bells were hung from limbs of trees. Poles were used to build corrals for the livestock. These buildings and corrals were surrounded by a stockade or pole fence for protection.

The first mission buildings were simple huts made of mud and sticks.

As soon as these **temporary** buildings and fences were completed, the padres showed the Indians how to build simple **irrigation** or water systems. The Indians built a dam of brush, earth, and rocks across a nearby stream and turned the water from the stream into an open ditch that had already been dug. The water ran through this ditch to the fields and to the temporary mission buildings. The padres also had the Indians clear the land around the mission. This land had to be cleared of trees, rocks, and brush so that the land could be plowed and prepared for planting. Wheat and corn were planted in the fields as well as orange, lemon, fig, and olive trees.

This stone-lined ditch once carried water to the mission in the distance.

PERMANENT MISSION BUILDINGS

After building the temporary mission shelters, starting water systems, and planting the first crops and orchards, the padres now planned to build sturdier mission structures. These new buildings were to be constructed around a main **patio** or courtyard. This arrangement of buildings was known as the **quadrangle**. The padres planned the quadrangle with care and although each mission had a different appearance, there was a definite pattern for the placement of the church, priests' quarters, unmarried women's quarters, kitchen, and homes for married couples.

1. Women's quarters (monjerio)
2. Tannery
3. Weavery
4. Pottery
5. Indian village
6. Storerooms
7. Workshops (school for Indians
8. Church
9. Baptistry (espadana)
10. Padres' quarters (convento)
11. Patio
12. Cemetery
13. Kitchen

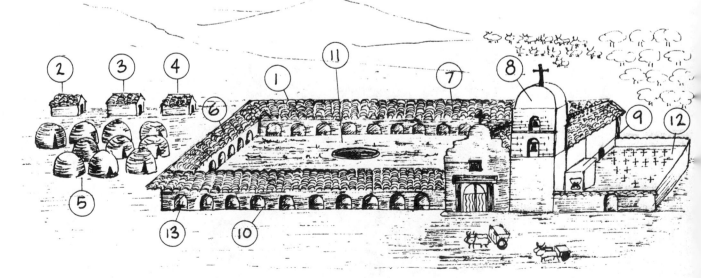

The missions were usually built in the shape of a quadrangle. There was a place for the church, padres' rooms, unmarried Indian women's rooms, kitchen, workshops, and storerooms.

ADOBE

Adobe soil was used to build the permanent mission buildings. A hole was dug in the ground and adobe soil and manure were thrown into the pit. Enough water was added to make a stiff mud. Then the Indians stepped into the pit and mixed the mud with their bare feet. The adobe mud was carried in leather buckets and poured into molds. The molds were lifted from the bricks and then the adobe bricks were left to dry in the sun. The Indians used these bricks to build the walls of the mission buildings.

PLASTER TO PROTECT ADOBE WALLS

Plaster was important when building mission structures. Lime plaster and lime **mortar** were made from **limestone** and seashells. The Indians collected pieces of limestone or seashells and heated them in special **kilns** made of adobe brick. These kilns heated the limestone or shells to a temperature of 1800 degrees until the limestone or shells became soft. The softened limestone and shells were called **quicklime**. The Indians mixed the quicklime with water to be used as mortar on the rock **foundations** of missions. Quicklime was also mixed with water and sand and used as a white plaster that the Indians spread over the adobe walls. When the plaster dried, it became hard and waterproof.

TILES

Roof tiles or **tejas** were not made until about ten years after the founding of the first mission in 1769. The clay mixture for the roof tiles was put into flat molds, then removed from the molds while still wet and shaped over half rounds of wood and dried. The dried roof tiles were then baked in a kiln for a long time. The long, slow baking of these tejas made them red, long-lasting, and fireproof.

Floor tiles or **ladrillos** were made with a stiffer, heavier mixture of clay than the mixture used for roof tiles. The clay was put into flat molds, the molds were lifted from the clay, and the floor tiles were left to dry in the sun. These tiles, like the roof tiles, were baked for a long time in kilns. Ladrillos were used for the flooring in the mission corridors and buildings of the quadrangle.

WATER SYSTEMS AT THE MISSIONS

Before the padres selected a site for a mission, they always made certain that there were nearby streams or rivers. Water was necessary at the mission for drinking, cooking, and washing. Water was also very important for the gardens, orchards, and crops of the mission. Often mission sites were changed in order to find better supplies of water.

After starting the permanent mission buildings, the first simple dams and water ditches dug by the padres and Indians were replaced with stone dams and stone-lined ditches. The stones and rocks in these **aqueducts** were held together by limestone mortar which made these water systems very sturdy and long-lasting.

The adobe mud was packed into wooden forms. When the mud was partly dry, the wooden form was lifted off. The adobe bricks were put in the sun until they were dry and hard. Each brick weighed about 60 pounds. One Indian worker could make 40 bricks a day.

When the adobe bricks had dried and were hard, the Indian workers were ready to build the mission. The walls of the mission were made of adobe bricks laid one row on top of another row. The walls were two or three feet thick.

These ladrillos have been walked upon by many people. Can you imagine the Indians and padres as they walked across this mission floor?

You may see the remains of this lime kiln at Mission San Juan Capistrano. This kiln was also used to melt tallow.

The roof tiles protected the adobe brick walls from the rainy weather. They were also fireproof.

Dogs were known to the California Indians before the coming of the Spanish people. In their mission journals the padres tell that dogs were very important because they helped to guard cattle, horses, and especially sheep. Dogs also helped to guard the drying adobe bricks and tiles as well as the fields and orchards.

At the missions there was even work for the cats. Many field mice invaded the mission storage rooms and nibbled at the sacks of corn and wheat. Cats were important to keep the mice from destroying the food supplies. In some of the missions you may still see cat-holes cut in the old doors so that the cats could move freely in and out of the mission. Today, you can still see cats roaming through mission gardens.

A SPANISH PADRE

I am a padre. I was born in Spain and came to the New World when I was nineteen years old. I came to the New World with a special purpose. I wanted to teach the Indians about my Christian God. The King of Spain paid for my voyage to the New World. I promised the king that I would serve for at least ten years as a missionary. Every padre who came to this new land made the same promise to the King of Spain.

I began my training as a missionary at a Franciscan college in Mexico City in New Spain. The Franciscan teachers at the college taught me special ways to work with the Indians. I had to memorize these three important rules: (1) be kind and friendly to the Indians, (2) encourage the Indians to help with work at the missions, and (3) reward the Indians with food and small gifts.

My first assignment was to teach the Indians at a mission in the Sierra Gorda Mountains in New Spain. The Spanish king had asked all of the padres to learn the Indians' languages. I worked hard to learn the Indian languages in the Sierra Gorda Mountains. Before long, I learned to speak several native **dialects**. As soon as I could talk to the Indians in their languages, I started to teach them my language. I showed the Indians how to take care of cattle, chickens, and other livestock. I worked with the Indians and built new workshops and storerooms at the mission. I showed the Indians how to plant wheat and corn. I liked teaching and working with these Indians and it helped prepare me for the time when I knew I would be sent to Alta California.

Several years later, I was assigned to work at the missions in Alta California. I went to Alta California with other padres and we looked forward to starting new missions. We followed the strict rules started by Father Serra and we taught the Christian religion to thousands of Alta California Indians. From early morning bells until evening prayers, we were very busy.

Now, I have been in the New World for 46 years. I have **devoted** my life to teaching and working with the Indians. I am proud to be a padre and I am proud to have helped Father Serra's dream come true.

BACKTRACKING

1. Give two reasons why the padres came to Alta California.

2. Give two reasons why the soldiers came to Alta California.

3. Why do you think tiles for mission roofs were made to replace tule and brush roofs?

BRAVE EXPLORERS

1. Pretend you are a padre about to start a mission in Alta California. Name three important things you would need to start a successful mission.

The Indians carved River of Life designs on the wooden mission doors.

The plows the Indians used were not very good. They were made from crooked limbs of trees. The men looked for trees that had two branches growing from the trunk. Then they cut down the tree and cut one of the branches short. They put an iron point on the end of that branch. The iron point was used to break the ground. The longer branch was used as a handle to guide the plow. The tree trunk was the tongue of the plow. Then the men shaped a long wooden bar called a yoke to fit on top of the heads of the oxen close between the horns. An Indian guided the plow as the oxen pulled it across the fields. It was necessary to plow the fields many times to break up the soil. This was very hard work!

CHAPTER TEN
MISSION LIFE

MISSION CROPS AND LIVESTOCK

MISSION CROPS

Crops, gardens, and orchards were started soon after the temporary shelters and water systems were built. First, good areas for gardens and fields had to be selected. Next, trees, shrubs, and brush had to be removed from the land. Then, the land needed to be **plowed**.

After the ground was plowed, the crops were planted. Wheat was planted by hand. Indians would take large handfuls of seed and as they walked along, they would scatter the seed over the plowed fields. Then the Indians tied long branches to the **yokes** of oxen. As the oxen dragged the branches over the fields, the loose dirt was pushed over the wheat seeds. The Indians planted corn by dropping several seeds into a hole and then used their feet to push and press down the soil over the seeds.

MISSION GARDENS

Every mission had a vegetable garden. The land for the gardens was prepared in the same manner as the fields were prepared. Beans, peas, squash, pumpkins, melons, red peppers, tomatoes, garlic, onions, and **herbs** grew in the mission gardens. Indian men, women, and children spent many hours weeding and hoeing these gardens.

Every mission had a vegetable garden. Some of the Indians planted their own gardens and shared their vegetables with other Indians.

MISSION ORCHARDS

Many kinds of fruit trees, including grapevines, were probably brought with the first expeditions to Alta California in 1769. After the land was cleared, **seedling** trees were planted. Large groups of orange, lemon, fig, pear, apricot, and peach trees grew well. Apple, plum, walnut, and almond trees also surrounded the missions. **Vineyards**, olive trees, and pomegranates were planted nearby. These were the beginnings of California's great farms and orchards.

Most of the missions had vineyards. Some vineyards were one acre in size while others were as large as 170 acres. The grapes were picked in late summer by the Indians at the mission and put into large **vats**. Young, strong Indian men crushed the grapes with their bare feet. The grape juice flowed out of an opening at the bottom of the vat into tubs or other containers. The juice was then **fermented** in barrels or pottery jars and when it became wine it was stored in dry, cool, dark rooms or cellars. Wine was used by the padres in many religious ceremonies.

CARING FOR THE MISSION CROPS, GARDENS, AND ORCHARDS

At first, gardens and fields were not fenced to keep out the livestock. The animals were guarded and kept away from the crops by the Indians. The Indian boys and girls watched the fields all day and sometimes all night. They threw stones and waved sticks at the cattle that got into the planted fields. As the number of livestock increased, it was necessary to fence the gardens and fields. Orchards, gardens, and vineyards were fenced with adobe walls, cactus hedges, or wide ditches.

Not only did the Indians have to care for and protect the gardens and fields of the missions, but many Indians had gardens of their own to care for. The Indians were encouraged by the padres to plant their own gardens and share the vegetables with their family and friends.

HARVESTING CORN

When the corn or **maize** was ripe, it was gathered from the stalks and carried to the mission in a **carreta**. The corn was **husked** by the Indians and stored on the cob in a storage room in the mission. Some of the corn kernels were saved to be planted the following year. Most of the corn was used for **atolé** or tortillas.

HARVESTING WHEAT

Wheat was harvested by many Indian workers who cut down the ripe grain with hand **sickles**. The cut wheat was gathered, loaded on carretas, and taken to the mission to be **threshed**. Each mission had a threshing floor. The cut wheat was piled on the floor and horses were used to trample the grain until it was separated from the wheat stalks. When the grain was separated from the wheat stalks, the horses were taken from the threshing room and the grain was then scooped from the floor by the Indians. Next, the grain had to be winnowed to remove bits of straw and **chaff**. The grain was then stored in the mission **granary**.

HARVESTING FRUITS AND VEGETABLES

Fruits and vegetables from the mission orchards and gardens were picked and stored in large leather bags or pottery storage jars. Sometimes fruits and vegetables were stored on shelves and covered with thick layers of clean, dry straw.

The Indians who planted, cared for, and harvested the crops of the missions were taught by the padres or by Indians who came with the padres from Baja California. The Indians worked long, hard hours for the padres, helping with the hundreds of jobs that would have been impossible for the padres to do by themselves.

The prickly pear cactus plants grew in thick hedges from 8 to 10 feet tall. They were often planted around the gardens and fields so that the livestock would not destroy the plants. These cactus plants also produced a sweet, pear-shaped fruit that the padres and Indians enjoyed eating.

The baking for the mission was done outdoors in a round beehive-like oven called a hornito. A fire was built inside the hornito. When the fire burned to ashes, the oven was ready for baking. Bread was baked inside and long paddles were used to take the bread from the oven.

Some Indians had the job of loading, hauling, and unloading wool, grain, grapes, corn, wheat, and stones in a carreta. Carretas were used constantly to carry goods back and forth from the fields to the missions and to other distant points.

When mission fields began producing large amounts of wheat, a gristmill was used to grind the grain. The grain was poured through a hole in the top grinding wheel. A burro was harnessed to a long pole and as the burro walked around the mill, the grain was ground between the two large round stones. Later, some gristmills were turned by water power instead of burros.

Olive trees were planted at many of the missions. The Indians picked the olives by hand from the lower branches of the trees. The olives near the top of the trees were knocked off with switches or shaken down by hitting the branches with poles. Indian children gathered the olives and put them into burden baskets. The Indian women carried the baskets of olives to the mill. The olives were poured into the mill and crushed by a large, flat stone that was turned by a blindfolded burro. When the olives were crushed, they were scooped from the mill, put into sacks made of strong **hemp** fiber and placed in an olive press. Two strong Indians worked the press and slowly the oil ran out of an opening at the bottom of the press into a tub. The oil was poured into jars and stored away. Olive oil was burned in church lamps, used as a medicine, and for cooking. Olive oil was even used for greasing machinery.

LIVESTOCK

Livestock was first brought to Alta California by the land and sea expeditions of Father Serra and Captain Portolá in the year 1769. As the first five missions were built, each was given eighteen head of cattle, four hogs, and some chickens.

The cattle were the most important livestock raised at the mission. They were large animals with long curving horns and sloping hind quarters. Cattle were **slaughtered** for **tallow**, hides, and meat. The cows gave a good supply of rich milk that could also be made into butter and cheese.

Sheep were also important. They provided the missions with meat as well as wool. The hogs provided **lard** for cooking and extra fat was used in soap-making. Sausages and hams were made from the hog meat. Horses were kept for riding purposes and seldom used for hauling or work in the fields.

Oxen were used for hard work. Mules were the pack animals and burros provided the power to turn the **gristmills**. Chickens were also raised at the missions. They provided meat as well as eggs.

Later, as the mission herds increased and the Indian neophytes became expert **vaqueros**, the herds of cattle, horses, and sheep were moved to ranchos several miles from the mission crops and fields. At each rancho, there were living quarters for the foreman, Indian vaqueros and their families. On these ranchos there were good pasture lands and water for the livestock. Here the cattle and horses were branded and the sheep were **ear marked**. Slaughtering cattle for tallow, hides, and meat and shearing sheep for wool took place on these ranchos. From these beginnings, grew the mission herds that became the great herds of California's livestock industry.

The Indians worked hard to build the missions, plant and harvest the mission crops, and care for the livestock. At each mission the Indian men, women, and children worked long hours. The padres taught the Indians how to do the many jobs, but without the Indians to do the work, the missions could never have come into being.

Herds of cattle came with the Spanish settlers over the land trails. The cattle lived on the plains surrounding the missions and ate the wild grasses. The land was so rich that the cattle had plenty of food.

When meat was needed for a mission, vaqueros went out on horses and lassoed a steer with a reata. The animal was brought in from the field and killed. It was cut up for meat and the meat was used as soon as possible. There were no refrigerators in those days, and there was no way of keeping fresh meat. Sometimes beef was cut into strips and dried in the same way the Indians had dried deer meat. This dried beef jerky was carried for food on journeys.

Cattle Brands of the California Missions

Name of Mission	Founded	Brand	Cattle
San Diego de Alcalá	1769	Ð	8,000
San Luis Rey de Francia	1798	5	26,000
San Juan Capistrano	1776	CAP	10,000
San Gabriel Arcángel	1771	₮	20,500
San Fernando Rey de España	1797	4	12,500
San Buena Ventura	1782	AB	17,300
Santa Barbara	1786	ঠ	3,600
Santa Inés	1804	৸	7,300
La Purísima Conceptión	1787	8	10,500
San Luis Obispo de Tolosa	1772	ℒ	8,600
San Miguel Arcángel	1797	3	9,000
San Antonio de Padua	1771	Ā	5,000
Nuestra Señora de la Soledad	1791	X	6,600
San Carlos Borromeo del Carmelo	1771	MR	2,050
San Juan Bautisto	1797	Ᾱ	11,000
Santa Cruz	1791	Â	3,500
Santa Clara de Assisí	1777	Á	9,000
San Jose de Guadelupe	1797	J	12,000
San Francisco de Assisí	1776	F	4,200
San Rafael Arcángel	1817	L	1,200
San Francisco de Solano	1823	F	2,500

Sannie '85

Cattle hides were scraped with knives to remove all the meat. Hides were washed and soaked in limestone water for 3 to 4 days. This process softened the cattle hide and made the hair loose. Hides were again scraped until all the hair was removed. Then hides were soaked in a tanning liquid for several months. When the hides were removed from this tanning liquid, they were washed again and then rubbed with grease and tallow to soften them. They were dried in the drying room and used for such things as sacks, saddles, shoes, boots, sandals, bridles, reins, and reatas.

When the mission herds of cattle and sheep grew large, the padres were able to trade tallow and hides with foreign ships that sailed along the coast of Alta California. Huge, black iron pots that had been used on whaling ships for melting whale fat, were traded to the padres. The padres used these large kettles to melt the tallow of the slaughtered steer and sheep from the mission herds.

In the springtime, wool was sheared from the sheep. It was carried to the mission where Indians removed burrs, sticks, and thorns from the sheep's wool. Then the wool was washed with soap in large kettles. All the grease was removed from the wool or the wool would not dye well. The wool was dried on bushes and pulled over brushes made of spiny seed pods to straighten the fibers. Then the wool was spun into long lengths of yarn.

The Indians and the padres of the missions wore clothing made of wool. The Indians wove the yarn into cloth. Looms were used to weave cloth. From the wool cloth, the Indians made blankets, loosely woven material for clothing, and coarse material for the padres' robes. Weaving was done by Indian men and women.

A CALIFORNIA MISSION INDIAN

Today, my day began at sunrise with the ringing of the Angeles Bells at the church. I went with the padres and the other Indians to the church for prayers. After prayers, a second bell called us to breakfast.

My mother and sister do most of the cooking for the people who live here at the mission. They had been cooking since before dawn and the steaming kettles of atolé smelled delicious. I spoke briefly with my friends as I stood in line waiting for my bowl to be filled with the hot mush. When breakfast was finished, a bell was rung and everyone went to their daily jobs.

Today, I helped plow the fields. Soon we will plant wheat. My father is the **mayordomo** and supervises all of the work done at the mission. He spent most of the day directing us as we prepared the fields for the wheat seed.

When the sun was high overhead, another bell called us together for the main meal of the day. I was very hungry and could hardly wait for my mother to serve the atolé. This time, she had added large chunks of meat and vegetables to the mush. My sister had spent the morning grinding corn and patting out tortillas. The warm tortillas tasted very good.

After the meal, it was time for a **siesta**. Everyone rests during this time. I found a shady place under the old grapevine that covered part of the mission porch. As I lay on the cool tiles, I thought about the time when the padres first came to our land.

The Indians in my village had come to the mission because we were curious and liked the gifts that were given to us by the padres. When we visited the mission, we listened patiently to the stories about God that the padres told us. Many of us understood the stories because we believe in God, but we call him by a different name. After we learned about the Christian God, the padres baptized us and made us members of the church. Now that we are baptized, the padres will not allow us to leave the mission. Some of my friends do not like this rule, but the padres are strict and will punish anyone who does not obey their rules. If we run away to escape from the mission, soldiers will be sent after us and bring us back to the mission. I have seen runaway Indians whipped or put in chains by the soldiers. The Spanish soldiers have caused us great unhappiness and most of us are afraid of the soldiers. The padres are usually kind to us. They see that we have food and shelter. As I thought about these things my eyes became heavy and soon I fell asleep.

After my siesta, I started back to the fields. As I walked down the long corridor, I could hear the clatter of the looms in the workshops. The weavers were spinning wool yarn into cloth. As I passed the kitchen, I could hear the hum of the women's voices as they began to prepare the evening meal. Beyond the mission walls, some Indian men were making adobe bricks. They mixed the mud and straw with their bare feet as they chanted an old Indian song.

That afternoon, I plowed the south field. Back and forth I walked until the soil was plowed to a fine, soft powder. This was hard work! Soon I noticed a welcome sight. A young Indian boy was bringing refreshment to us. Today, he carried a large clay jar filled with cool water. A little vinegar had been added to the water to **quench** our thirsts and honey added a wonderfully sweet taste to the drink.

In the late afternoon we were called to the evening meal by the ringing of a bell. This meal was the same as breakfast. Then, another bell called us all to prayers. When our prayers were finished, we spent the evening playing games, singing, and talking.

I spent most of this evening listening to the padres tell us about guests who will soon visit the mission. This is always an exciting time. The padres are planning a grand **fiesta** in honor of the guests. There will be much food. A cow and a hog will be slaughtered and roasted over an open fire. There will be stacks of warm tortillas and large bowls filled with beans and vegetables. Dancing and singing will go on long into the night.

As I sit here listening to the plans for the fiesta, I think about when I was a boy and lived with my tribe in a small village deep in the forest. How different my life is now! I think of my friends who still live in the forest. Perhaps, someday, I may join them and live, once again, the life of a free Indian!

Soap was made by using extra fats which could not be used for anything else. Water was poured through wood ashes to make a liquid lye. The melted fat and liquid lye were boiled in large kettles and the soft soap which floated to the top as it cooled was skimmed off. The soft soap was put into a mold, cut into bars, and dried on a shelf. At one time, there were large kettles for making soap in the brick-lined pits you see in the above picture.

BACKTRACKING

1. What type of area would you look for if you were in charge of starting mission gardens, orchards, and crops?

2. How do you think the first fruit trees were brought to Alta California? How were the trees kept alive?

3. Name three ways the livestock were kept away from the gardens, crops, and orchards.

4. What do you think the missions would have been like if the Indians had not helped the padres?

BRAVE EXPLORERS

1. What is the difference between a mule and a burro?

Candles were made by boiling the extra tallow from cattle in huge iron kettles. The Indians stirred the tallow in the large kettles, then allowed the tallow to cool and become solid. One method of making candles was on a candle wheel. Pieces of string were hung from a big candle wheel and the wheel was turned slowly as melted tallow was poured over the strings. This was repeated many times until the candles were thick. The candles were then cut from the candle wheel and stored.

Some missions had orchestras with ten, twenty, or more Indians. The musicians played violins, cellos, horns, and flutes.

130

CHAPTER ELEVEN
MUSIC AT THE MISSIONS

CALIFORNIA INDIAN MUSIC

The California Indians had songs for almost everything they did. They sang when they played games or held special ceremonies. They sang for good luck in hunting and fishing and they also sang for a good acorn crop. Happy Indian voices sang in rhythm to the thumping sounds of stone **pestles** as acorns were ground into flour. Singing was an important part of the California Indians' lives.

Sometimes, when the California Indians sang, they did special dances. In their dances, the Indians acted out what they wanted to say. Some of the dances went on for many days. The men, women, and children enjoyed these dances and every Indian child learned the songs and dances of his or her own tribe.

CALIFORNIA MISSION MUSIC

When the Spanish came to Alta California, the Indians were fascinated by the **chants** and songs of the padres. The padres found that their religious music attracted many Indians to the missions. Music was important to all the Franciscan padres and through their music, the padres began to teach the Indians the Christian religion. Because the Indians loved music, they quickly learned the chants and songs that the padres taught them. The music of the padres and the music of the California Indians blended together and soon the missions along the *El Camino Reál* were filled with the pleasant sounds of Indian choirs, orchestras, and mission bells.

Padre Durán had Indian musicians accompany the choir. The musicians helped the singers stay in time with the music.

These California Indians at Mission San José are dressed and painted for an important native ceremony. The dancers' bodies are decorated with tattoos, and stripes of red, black, and white body paint. One Indian is covered with feathers held in place with tar. The Indian on the far right painted his body to look like he is wearing a soldier's jacket and boots. During the dance the Indians would take glowing coals from a fire and put them in their mouths.

Mission music stands had to be strong to hold the large heavy choir books.

The music books used at the missions were very large so that everyone in the choir and orchestra could read the notes easily. Many padres wrote music for their choirs.

For more than sixty-five years, the lives of everyone in California, Indians as well as Spaniards, were regulated by the ringing of mission bells. The bells called the people to work, to prayers, and announced the happenings of the day.

The ringing of the mission bells was an honor that the Indians loved. A few Indians still rang the bells in abandoned mission churches long after the mission period had come to a close.

The joyous ringing of the mission bells announced the coming and going of padres and visitors. The bells were also rung to tell of special events, festivals, weddings, and baptisms.

A CALIFORNIA INDIAN BELL RINGER

I am the Indian who watched Father Serra ring the bell the day the good padre first started Mission San Antonio de Padua. I remember the day that I heard the bell ringing and ringing, calling me to the Valley of the Oaks not too far away from my village. I ran to the valley and there on one of the oak trees hung a large round-shaped object. The padre was pulling a rope and the large object was making a noise. Later, the padre told me that the object was called a bell. The padre showed me how to ring the bell softly and how to ring the bell loudly. I was so happy that I wanted to go and tell my family about the bell. The padre gave me gifts of beads and dried fruit to take back to my village.

The next day, I returned with several people from my village who wanted to see the padre and the large bell. The padre let each of us ring the bell. He gave us more gifts. Later that day, we helped the padre gather branches to build a shelter. We returned each day to see the padre and the bell and help the padre with his chores.

Now, I live at Mission San Antonio de Padua. The padre has made me the official bell ringer. My arms and shoulders are very strong from ringing the bell. I ring the bell early in the morning for prayers before breakfast. I ring the bell again at noon and for siesta time. I ring the bell for the evening meal and the evening prayers.

I can make the mission bell move back and forth and I can also make the bell turn completely over! To get the bell to turn over, I push the bell with the palms of both of my hands. Then I grab the top of the bell yoke and give a great pull downward until the bell is upside down. With a great heave, I send the bell spinning around and around. What a joyous sound the bell makes when it is rung like this, but I must be very careful not to be hit by the bell as it is very heavy.

Music is a very important part of our mission. The padres enjoy music and they like teaching us to play the flutes and string instruments. Many of the Indian boys play flutes or violins in the orchestra and many boys sing in the choir. My mother and sisters love the songs we sing in church, but for me the songs of the bell that I ring will always be the best!

A CALIFORNIA INDIAN MUSICIAN

I am a mission Indian. I was born here at the mission. When I was very small my mother taught me the songs of our tribe. She taught me the songs for men's games and dances, songs for women's games and dances, songs for wartime, hunting songs, songs for the ill or the dead, and songs for storytelling. I love the music and dances of my tribe. At special times, the Indians here at the mission sing and dance some of our special music for others to see and hear.

As a young boy I loved to listen to the Indian choir singing church hymns. Some of the Indians played violins and flutes to help the choir stay on key and sing in **unison**. One day as I listened and sang softly to myself, the padre noticed me and called me to him. He asked me to sing along with the other Indian neophytes. I looked at a large book with colored notes that told me when to sing higher or lower. As I started to sing, I found I could follow the colored notes quite easily. If the colored notes that I followed in the large book moved up a few lines, I made my voice go up too. If the colored notes moved down the lines, I made my voice go down. Our Indian choir sings two, three, and sometimes four parts. Everyone in the mission likes to listen to our music.

The padre is teaching me how to play the drums so that I can keep better time with the Indian choir. It is easy for me to learn how to play this drum because my own father taught me to play a foot drum when I was very small. I am teaching several Indian boys to play the drums so that they too may join the Indian orchestra when they are older.

Music has always been a part of my life here at the mission. I am glad the padres love music as much as the Indians love music!

Young Indian women at the Pala Mission played mandolins and guitars in the
year 1905.

BACKTRACKING

1. The California Indians sang when they played games. Give two more examples of when the California Indians sang.

2. Why did the padres teach music to the Indians?

3. Why were the music books at the mission so large?

4. Padre Durán had Indian musicians who played horns and violins to accompany the choir. How did the musicians help the singers?

5. Give three reasons why bells were important to life at the missions.

BRAVE EXPLORERS

1. Why do you think the singing and dancing of the California Indians sometimes went on for many days?

The Peralta family helped to start the planned pueblo of San José. The Peralta adobe can be seen today in busy downtown San José.

CHAPTER TWELVE
PUEBLOS AND POBLADORES

THE SAN JOSÉ PUEBLO

A few months after the Santa Clara mission had been founded in 1777, Governor Felipe de Neve of Alta California chose a place to begin the first **pueblo** or town, named El Pueblo de San José de Guadalupe. San José was the first California settlement to be built as a planned town! Each of the other settlements had started as a mission or presidio.

This first pueblo was built by soldiers. Each soldier and family was given ten dollars a month, a piece of land in the new town, plus two oxen, two cows, two sheep, two goats, tools, and seeds. Some thirty-seven square miles of land was set aside for the San José pueblo. This seems like a lot of land for the few **pobladores** that started the pueblo, but everyone hoped that San José would grow.

THE LOS ANGELES PUEBLO

Governor Neve was very pleased with the way things were going in California. He wanted to set up more towns like San José. The governor decided upon another place to build a second pueblo. Governor Neve remembered that the great explorer, Gaspár de Portolá, had talked about a wide plain near the San Gabriel mission. The governor liked the idea of building a town on this wide plain. Governor Neve decided to name this new pueblo, El Pueblo de Nuestra Señora de los Angeles. This pueblo was started in September, 1781. Governor Neve had a great deal of difficulty finding families to come to California to build the Los Angeles pueblo. Finally, eleven families came up the long trail from Baja California. There were Indian, Black, and Spanish pobladores.

MORE PUEBLOS ALONG THE COLORADO RIVER

Juan Bautista de Anza had opened a trail from Sonora in New Spain through the Colorado River area. That trail led across the mountains and deserts to Mission San Gabriel. Two missions and pueblos were planned to be built along Anza's trail beside the Colorado River. There were many villages of Yuma Indians in this area. The Spanish officials thought that the pobladores going to California could rest at these new pueblos and make the long journey easier.

In 1780 and 1781, many families and soldiers moved to the sites of these new pueblos near the Yuma villages. Unfortunately, the new Spanish settlers took over the land along the Colorado River that belonged to the Yuma Indians. The new settlers did not respect the rights of the Indians. The settlers allowed their livestock to eat and destroy the native plants that the

Indians used for food. The Indians were mistreated by the Spanish soldiers. The Indians began to dislike the Spanish settlers. One day the Indians attacked the new settlers and destroyed the pueblos. The pueblos were never rebuilt and Spanish settlers no longer came to Alta California along Anza's trail that crossed the Colorado River.

The pobladores living in the pueblos grew large fields of wheat. They ground the wheat in gristmills. Much of the ground wheat was sent to the soldiers and their families living at the presidios.

Some of the California Indians learned to use a rip-saw to cut boards for buildings.

UNPLANNED PUEBLOS

Spanish officials often brought pobladores from New Spain to start planned pueblos. There were, however, several unplanned pueblos that were started by the soldiers who finished their work at the presidios and stayed in the area with their families. Unplanned pueblos started near the presidios of San Diego, Monterey, San Francisco, and Santa Barbara. Another unplanned pueblo was at Sonoma, north of San Francisco Bay.

None of the pueblos grew very large because the Spanish officials did not allow trading with other countries. Spain had now established its claim in Alta California, but most of California still was a land of little Indian villages.

A busy kitchen

An unplanned pueblo started near the presidio of San Francisco.

LUIS MARÍA PERALTA

I, Luis María Peralta, came to Alta California with my parents, brothers, and sister in the year 1776. Our expedition was led by the great explorer Juan Bautista de Anza. I was sixteen years old and learned many things about exploring on that expedition! I remember the old padre, Padre Font, who kept a diary of all happenings on this exciting journey. He was my friend and we often talked for hours. When I was 17 years old, I became a soldier and helped guard and build some of the presidios and missions in northern California.

Now, 46 years later, I am the **comisionado** of the pueblo of San José. As comisionado I have many duties. One of my most important duties is to make sure the people of the pueblo follow the laws. When I first came to this pueblo, 15 years ago, there were many problems. People did not want to work and often fights broke out in the streets. Now, things are much better. The people work hard and our fields supply enough food to the presidios of San Francisco and Monterey to feed all the soldiers and their families.

I live with my wife, María Loreto Alviso and my nine children in our small adobe in San José. My wife is a good mother and works very hard. I have sent my four sons to school to learn to read and write. I am strict with my children, but kind. My children respect me and I am proud of them.

This year, 1822, I will retire from the office of comisionado. The Spanish officials have granted me over 40,000 acres of land as a reward for my many years of military service in Alta California. I will name my land Rancho San Antonio. It is one of the most valuable and largest land grants ever given to a person in Alta California! I am honored and someday I shall divide this land among my sons. Although I will now be able to build a large rancho, I think I would prefer to live in my comfortable little adobe. I will let my sons build great ranchos and I will live a simple life like I have lived since I came to this beautiful land of California.

MARÍA LORETO ALVISO PERALTA

When I, María Loreto Alviso, was five years old I traveled to Alta California with my family. We came with the expedition led by the famous pathfinder Juan Bautista de Anza. Also, on this very same expedition was the Peralta family. I did not know it then, but eight years later I would marry Luis María Peralta.

The journey to Alta California was very long and many times I thought we would never see the land of California. When we crossed the deserts, it was so hot that it was hard to breathe. As we crossed the mountains, the cold snow-covered lands made it difficult for the oxen to pull our wagon. I remember how my fingers and toes ached from the icy weather. When we finally saw the beautiful grassy plain and the sparkling white walls of Mission San Gabriel, we were overjoyed. The padres and the Indians were very surprised to see us. They treated us very well and the next day a great fiesta was held in our honor.

My family moved on to San Francisco. We were among the very first settlers in the San Francisco Bay Area.

When I was thirteen, I married Luis María Peralta. My husband was a soldier and we moved many times. We lived in the barracks at the presidios. Life was difficult in those early days. The land was still very wild and each day I worked very hard cleaning our dusty rooms, cooking, washing, and caring for my babies.

In 1807, 23 years after we were married, Luis was appointed as comisionado of the pueblo of San José. Finally, we could settle down in one place. We lived in a small adobe house near the center of the pueblo. Here, our nine children could live a happy life.

Now, I am a grandmother and great-grandmother. I tell my grandchildren about my young life in Alta California. They tell me that I was a very brave and courageous woman to have been one of the first pioneers in a new and wild frontier.

JOSÉ VANEGAS

I am one of the "Founding Forty-Four". I am José Vanegas. In February, 1781, my wife, Maxima Aguilar, and I plus 42 other pobladores left Alamos, Sonora in New Spain to travel to Alta California. Together, the forty-four of us began the second pueblo, El Pueblo de Nuestra Señora de los Angeles.

Governor de Neve had asked that Spanish families start this pueblo near San Gabriel to grow more grains, fruits, and vegetables for the soldiers and families living in Alta California.

When we arrived in Alta California, we began clearing the land for the plaza and fields of this new pueblo. This was a big job. Every man, woman, and child worked very hard and soon the buildings around the plaza were started. Fields were plowed and wheat was planted. The governor was pleased with our progress and I was named the first **alcalde** of Los Angeles.

As alcalde, I had many duties. I had to see that everyone obeyed the law and did their share of work. If there were arguments over land or supplies, I settled them. I had to be strict, but fair.

I am also a farmer. On our rancho, my wife and I grew grain and raised cattle. We have one son. His name is Cosme. When Cosme was a young boy, he loved to watch the soldiers. Now, that he is older, he has enlisted as a soldier at the Santa Barbara Presidio. He is a good soldier and together with the other soldiers, they protect the people at the mission and in our small pueblo.

Four years ago, after my wife died, I left the pueblo of Los Angeles. I moved south and became the mayordomo at the missions in San Diego and San Luis Rey.

I have heard that the little pueblo of Los Angeles is growing larger each day. More and more Spanish settlers are coming to Alta California. I often think of those days long ago when I worked hard to start the first adobes in Los Angeles. I know that some day this pueblo that had such a humble beginning will become an important settlement in Alta California.

BACKTRACKING

1. Name the first and second pueblos in Alta California. Where were they located?

2. The Spanish settlers started pueblos along the Colorado River near the villages of the Yuma Indians. Why did Spanish officials feel that this area would be a good place to start pueblos?

3. What did the pobladores in the new pueblos along the Colorado River do to upset the Yuma Indians?

4. What is the difference between a planned and unplanned pueblo?

BRAVE EXPLORERS

1. After 1781, Spanish people no longer used Anza's trail to come to Alta California. Why do you think this happened?

The small planned pueblo of Los Angeles started in 1781 has grown into one of the largest cities in the United States!

Mission Santa Barbara today

CHAPTER THIRTEEN
MORE LINKS IN THE MISSION CHAIN

THE TENTH LINK

In December, 1786, Mission Santa Barbara was founded by the new president of the Alta California missions, Father Fermín Francisco de Lasuén. Once the site for this mission was chosen, it was never changed. The first temporary structures were built like a log cabin and surrounded by a wooden stockade for protection.

The first buildings were a chapel, living quarters for the padres, a kitchen, and storerooms. Later, more permanent buildings of adobe were started and two nearby creeks were dammed with solid sandstone. From these dams, workers built several miles of sandstone aqueducts. These aqueducts carried the water to two **reservoirs** that were on a hillside near the mission. From these reservoirs, the water was carried to the mission, corrals, fields, and orchards. The fountain and **lavandería** near the mission's main entrance were connected with this water system.

Many Indians came to live at Mission Santa Barbara. As more Indians came, the mission church was made larger and more buildings were added. In 1812, a terrible earthquake damaged all the mission buildings and the padres lived in temporary shelters for almost three years. Then in 1815, a new stone church was built. Father Ripoll planned this church and José Ramírez was the master-mason for this stone church. Father Ripoll, José Ramírez, and the Indians worked for five years until the great stone church was completed.

This is Mission Santa Barbara as it looked in 1865. If you look carefully at the left side of the mission, you will see the fountain that is still at the mission today.

FATHER LASUÉN

I am Father Fermín Francisco de Lasuén. I was born in Spain in 1736 and came to New Spain in 1761. I served in the Baja California missions and then I was asked to travel to Alta California to serve with Father Serra.

My first years in California were not happy ones. My friend, Father Jayme, was killed at Mission San Diego. The Indians at that mission did not like the padres or the soldiers and when I was assigned to be the new padre at San Diego mission, I knew I would not be able to show my unhappiness if I wanted to bring Indians to the mission.

Father Serra wrote many letters of encouragement to me at San Diego. He praised my kind ways and told me to remain quiet and calm in all things.

My Indian brothers and I have built a new church here and I have baptized the thousandth Indian. I would like to baptize more Indians, but there always seems to be unrest at this mission. Perhaps, our Indians are unsettled because other Indians come close by here on their travels to and from the ocean. These Indians tell our Indians to leave the mission.

On August 28, 1784, I received the news that my friend, Father Serra, had died. What a saint Father Serra was. I shall miss his letters and words of encouragement to me.

Soon a great honor came to me. I was to be the new President of the Alta California Missions. For the next eighteen years I worked hard to establish nine more missions. The number of missionaries went from 18 to 40, baptisms increased from 7,000 to 37,000, Indians living at the missions increased from 5,000 to 18,000, **produce** from the fields increased from 15,000 **fanegas** to 48,000 fanegas, and cattle increased from 5,000 head to 77,000 head.

Father Serra had laid the groundwork for all of these things to happen and I am proud to have continued on with his work!

Father Virgilio Biasiol is the director of the Santa Barbara Mission Archives Library. He is holding a journal written by Father Junípero Serra.

JUANA MARÍA

I am Juana María, an Indian woman. I have lived alone for many years on San Nicolás Island. This island is one of the Channel Islands not far off the coast from a great mainland the Spanish call Alta California.

Years ago a ship came to take away all of the Indians that lived on my island. We were going to be taken to the Alta California coast where we were to live with many other Indians at Mission Santa Barbara. Although I was already on board the ship, I jumped overboard and went back to the island to get my brother who had wandered away and was left behind. By the time I reached my brother, a terrible storm had started and the ship had to leave without us.

Soon after, my brother died and I lived alone for eighteen years. I hunted seal and fished for sea bass with arrows and hooks I made from rocks and bones. I made my own clothing from seal skins. I used bone needles and **sinew** to sew the skins together. I am strong and I learned to survive alone.

Now, men have come to take me in their ship to live in a new place with many people. As the ship sails away, I watch my island grow smaller and smaller. I shall never forget the many years that I lived alone on San Nicolás Island.

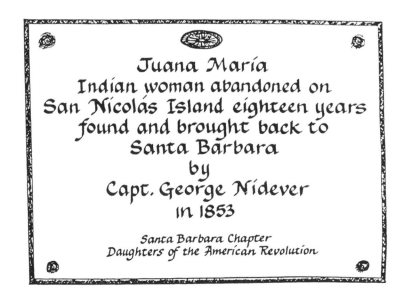

Juana María
Indian woman abandoned on
San Nicolás Island eighteen years
found and brought back to
Santa Bárbara
by
Capt. George Nidever
in 1853

Santa Barbara Chapter
Daughters of the American Revolution

LA PURÍSIMA CONCEPCIÓN

La Purísima Concepción is located half way between Santa Barbara and San Luis Obispo. This mission was founded by Father Lasuén on December 8, 1787. It had a good beginning and Indians from nearby villages came to the mission.

Several years later, the walls of the mission had to be strengthened and rebuilt. By 1802, the Indians had built a fine adobe church, workshops, and many small adobe houses for themselves. Then the earthquakes and floods of 1812 ruined all the buildings. The padres requested and received permission from the Spanish officials to **relocate** Mission La Purísima to a better spot across the river. The people at Mission La Purísima had many problems, such as earthquakes, floods, fires, **droughts**, and diseases. Even with all these problems, La Purísima became a successful mission because of the **faithfulness** of the Indians and padres.

Mission La Purísima as it looks today

Like all the missions, Mission La Purísima had a water system that provided water for cooking, washing, and irrigating the crops. Water was brought to the fountains and lavanderías of the mission by aqueducts and clay pipes. This photograph, taken in 1890, shows the remains of the mission and one of the lavanderías.

Fountain at Mission La Purísima

THE TWELFTH MISSION, SANTA CRUZ

The site for the Santa Cruz mission, like the other missions, was selected because of good climate, soil, fresh water, and friendly Indians. The Santa Cruz area had been known since 1769 when Father Crespí passed through this area with an exploration party. In his diary, Father Crespí told about the giant trees with reddish bark and timber. Father Crespí named these trees Redwood Trees. Father Palóu in 1776 on his way to San Francisco also mentioned that Santa Cruz had every possible thing a mission required: ". . . good land, water, pasture, firewood, and timber." Because of these good reports about the Santa Cruz area, Father Lasuén founded Mission Santa Cruz on August 28, 1791.

The Indians began cutting timber and the padres decided where the buildings would be placed. Horses, cattle, and mules were sent from other missions. By the end of 1796, the mission church had been built of stone and adobe and the mission had a mill and ground its own grain. The mission, however, was miles off the *El Camino Reál* so few visitors came to Santa Cruz mission. The padres found that the Indians in this area had plenty of wild game, seeds, and berries and were not interested in living at the mission. The number of Indians at the mission was never more than 523, the fewest neophytes at any of the missions.

To add to these problems, Spanish officials started a pueblo named Branciforte near the mission. The padres had always been against having presidios and pueblos near the missions. The padres felt that the people who lived in these settlements would be a bad influence on the Indians. The pueblo of Branciforte was started in the summer of 1797 and it caused many unfortunate problems for the padres and Indians. Crafty and untruthful people mistreated the Indians and padres and this led to the downfall of Mission Santa Cruz. The mission that began so well, ended poorly.

This painting shows what Mission Santa Cruz might have looked like when it was completed in 1794. Two years later the pueblo of Branciforte was built not far from the San Lorenzo River that flowed in front of the mission.

In 1857, the old church at Mission Santa Cruz collapsed. Two strong earth-quakes had weakened the building. This painting was done soon after the church collapsed. When the mission was restored in 1889, this picture was the only record of the inside of the church.

As recently as 1954, Mission Soledad was nothing more than crumbled adobe walls.

MISSION SOLEDAD

The thirteenth mission, Nuestra Señora de la Soledad, was founded by Father Lasuén on October 9, 1791. This mission was named for Our Lady of Solitude. The site for this mission was about three miles inland from the *El Camino Reál* in a lovely, quiet valley. The weather was very hot in the summer and cold and damp in the winter. Many of the padres who came to this mission disliked the climate and the loneliness of the valley. Because of the cold winters, many padres had **rheumatism** and lung diseases. Almost thirty padres came and left the mission during its early years!

During the first years, the mission did fairly well. Crops and livestock were plentiful and at one time the mission had around 600 neophytes. Father Florencio Ibañez spent fifteen years at Mission Soledad, the longest of any padre at this mission. He liked to teach the Indians music and often wrote plays for them.

By 1824, earthquakes, floods, and **epidemics** had started to ruin the mission. Father Vicente Francisco de Sarría came to help. This lonely mission, however, was now too poor to produce enough food for the few Indians that lived there. Soon Father Sarría died of starvation and the few remaining Indians carried him to Mission San Antonio de Padua for burial. The Indians then left, never to return to Mission Soledad.

COMMODORE HIPOLITO BOUCHARD

I am Commodore Hipolito Bouchard. I was born in France and I have always loved the sea. I have spent many years in South America and am the captain of two ships, the *Santa Rosa* and the *Argentina*. My ships are well equipped with guns and cannons. The Spanish people often call me a pirate, but I prefer to call myself a daring seaman.

My greatest adventure took place in the year 1818. My plan was to attack and rob the missions and settlements along the Alta California coast. When the people of Alta California heard I was coming, all four presidios were alerted. Women and children were told by Governor Sola to pack all their valuables and hide in the hills. The men were told to stay and help the soldiers defend the missions and towns. I can just imagine the confusion and fear I caused! I laughed when I heard that the men were gathering all their guns and artillery to frighten me away! What could these silly people do against me, the great Bouchard?

I was especially interested in Monterey, the capital of Alta California. I had heard that this town had many houses, large herds of cattle and sheep, and storage rooms filled with wheat, wool, hides, and other goods.

When my ships entered the bay of Monterey, I was greeted by Commandante Estudillo who stood on the shore and called to me through a silver **megaphone**, "Ho, Brigantine! What ship is that?" I answered this question by firing my guns.

The battle was on! During this battle, one of my ships was badly damaged, but it did not matter to me! I was still able to land my other ship and I led my 600 armed men into Monterey, the grand capital of Alta California. We took complete possession of Monterey.

We left Monterey and sailed down the coast of Alta California. I decided to raid Rancho del Refugio, a very rich rancho near Santa Barbara. Unfortunately, during the attack, several of my men were **lassoed** and captured by the vaqueros who worked at this rancho. The people of Santa Barbara refused to release my men unless I promised to leave Alta California.

We are now sailing peacefully along the coast of South America. I laugh when I think of all the fear and excitement I caused in those quiet, sleepy towns of Alta California. I truly am a daring seaman!

BACKTRACKING

1. Name the padre who became the new president of the Alta California missions after Father Serra's death.

2. The lavandería at Mission Santa Barbara is still located near the mission. What was the lavandería used for?

3. Mission La Purísima was totally destroyed by floods and earthquakes and had to be rebuilt in a new location. The padres and Indians were hardworking. Name one more characteristic of these people and tell why you think this characteristic is an important one.

4. Why didn't more Indians come to the Santa Cruz Mission?

5. What was the name of the pueblo built near the Santa Cruz Mission? Why didn't the padres want this pueblo to be built near the mission?

BRAVE EXPLORERS

1. What are some interesting things that happened at the thirteenth mission, Mission Nuestra Señora de la Soledad?

Mission Soledad

Tammie Ahlberg, a young explorer, at beautiful Mission Santa Inés

CHAPTER FOURTEEN
COMPLETING THE MISSION CHAIN

TWO YEARS AND FIVE MISSIONS!

The years 1797 and 1798 were very important to the California mission chain. During these years five more missions were founded! These new mission links strengthened the mission chain that connected San Diego to San Francisco. The Franciscan padres had always hoped to have enough missions along the *El Camino Reál* so that at the end of each day the weary traveler would have a place to rest.

The Spanish officials had not allowed Father Lasuén to start a new mission since Missions Santa Cruz and Soledad had been founded six years before. The Spanish officials had felt that starting more missions would cost too much money. After many discussions, Father Lasuén was finally given permission to start new missions. Father Lasuén was so overjoyed that he planned five new missions in the years 1797 and 1798.

MISSION SAN JOSÉ

Mission San José, the fourteenth mission, was founded by Father Lasuén on June 11, 1797. This mission was located fifteen miles from the San José pueblo along the *El Camino Reál*. By the end of 1797, the padres had only 33 neophytes living at the mission, but within three years there were about 300 neophytes at the mission. By 1824, almost two thousand Indians were making their homes at Mission San José.

Mission San José had 20,000 acres of land, 15,000 head of cattle and its huge fields produced great quantities of grains, fruits, and vegetables. Mission San José became one of the most successful missions in Northern California.

One of the oldest known photographs of any mission is this photograph of Mission San José in 1852.

Rebuilding Mission San José

The Bullard family is exploring the rebuilt Mission San José.

MISSION SAN JUAN BAUTISTA

About two weeks after Father Lasuén founded Mission San José, he selected and blessed a site for the fifteenth mission, Mission San Juan Bautista. This mission was located in a beautiful valley filled with oak trees. From the very beginning, Mission San Juan Bautista was a success. The friendly Indians helped to build an adobe church, barracks, granary, and adobe houses. Soon the church was much too small for the many neophytes who came to the mission. The padres could not decide if they should make the old church larger or build a new church. Their problem was solved when a series of earthquakes damaged the church as well as many buildings. Now, the padres decided that as they rebuilt the church they would make it larger.

As more Indians came to the mission, the padres decided to build an even larger church. In 1808, a new padre, Father Felipe del Arroyo de la Cuesta, arrived at Mission San Juan Bautista. He decided that the larger church should have three aisles because he expected the Indian population to continue to increase. He wanted a church big enough to hold 1,000 people. Unfortunately, the Indian population began to grow smaller instead of larger. In 1805, there were 1,100 neophytes living at the mission. In 1812, there were only 600 neophytes. Many Indians had died from the white man's diseases. Because there were not enough Indians living at the mission, Father la Cuesta closed off two of the aisles of the church.

Father la Cuesta and Father Estévan Tápis worked to bring more Indians to the mission. Father Tápis was a great musician and because of his Indian choir and music, more Indians came to Mission San Juan Bautista. Father la Cuesta was a great scholar. He was very interested in the Indian way of life and learned thirteen different Indian dialects. Perhaps, because of his great interest in the Indians, the Indian population at Mission San Juan Bautista grew.

San Juan Bautista in 1931

This photograph of Mission San Miguel was taken before the year 1900. Look carefully for the big bell in the wooden frame in front of the church. It weighed 2,500 pounds!

The largest bell in the campanario is the same bell that once hung in the wooden frame in front of the church of Mission San Miguel. You can see this campanario in back of the church.

SAN MIGUEL ARCÁNGEL

The summer of 1797 was a very busy one for Father Lasuén. He had founded Mission San José and Mission San Juan Bautista in June and then on July 25, 1797, he founded the sixteenth mission, San Miguel Arcángel.

When Father Lasuén, padres, and soldiers first arrived to found Mission San Miguel, a group of friendly Indians welcomed them and helped them set up camp. That first day, fifteen Indians asked Father Lasuén to baptize them. In time, a small adobe church and living quarters were built. A fence of sticks and brush surrounded these buildings.

San Miguel, like the other missions, had its share of troubles. The summer heat was so great that the padres often became ill. It is said that even the flies and fleas died of the heat. During these hot months, the nearby streams and water supplies dried up. Crops died and the livestock suffered. A terrible fire in 1806 almost completely ruined the church, workshops, and storerooms. Many bushels of grain and large supplies of wool were destroyed.

Father Juan Martín was the padre at Mission San Miguel for 27 years. He learned the Indian language very well. He was responsible for having the church and mission workshops rebuilt after the fire of 1806.

By 1824, there had been 2,300 Indian baptisms at Mission San Miguel. About 900 Indians were living at the mission. The land holdings of Mission San Miguel were large. The pastures, fields, and orchards stretched 50 miles to the north and south of the mission. The two padres at the mission depended upon the Indians to take care of these large holdings. Like most of the missions, San Miguel had small ranchos miles from the mission where Indians were in charge of looking after the fields and herds of livestock.

SAN FERNANDO REY DE ESPAÑA

During the late summer of 1797, Father Lasuén founded another mission. This was the fourth mission he had founded within four months! Father Lasuén founded Mission San Fernando Rey de España on September 8, 1797. The site for this mission was between Missions San Buenaventura and San Gabriel on a rancho once owned by Francisco Reyes, the alcalde of the Los Angeles pueblo. Father Lasuén and Father Dumetz found the Indians very friendly and on the day of the founding, several Indian children were brought to be baptized.

The mission grew and within nine years a new larger church was built. When this new church at San Fernando Rey was completed, there was a great celebration. Indian musicians from Missions Santa Barbara and La Purisíma played their instruments and sang beautiful songs. These excellent Indian musicians were the highlight of the celebration.

Mission San Fernando Rey de España produced hides, tallow, soap, cloth, grapes, dates, and olives as well as other mission products. Many of these products were sold to people living in the growing pueblo of Los Angeles. This mission also became a very popular stopping place for travelers on the *El Camino Reál*.

By 1900, most of Mission San Fernando Rey had fallen into ruins. In the late 1930's, the Southwest Museum of Los Angeles began to rebuild this mission. Look carefully at the end of the mission corridor and you will see a post. Mission bell posts like this one were placed at several of the missions.

Father Fermín Francisco de Lasuén became the president of the Alta California missions after the death of Father Serra. Like Father Serra, he too started nine missions in Alta California.

SAN LUIS REY DE FRANCIA

The last mission that Father Lasuén founded was San Luis Rey de Francia on June 13, 1798. This was the eighteenth mission. During its best years, the mission was surrounded by thirty square miles of orchards, gardens, and fields of grain. Indian neophytes took care of thousands of cattle and sheep.

Father Antonio Peyri was with Father Lasuén at the founding of Mission San Luis Rey. Father Peyri was 29 years of age and he stayed at this mission for 34 years! Under his guidance, San Luis Rey became one of the most successful missions along the *El Camino Reál*. Seven thousand baptisms were recorded in the mission journals and by 1826 there were 4,000 Indian neophytes living and working at the mission.

A painting of San Luis Rey de Francia in 1827

Father Peyri, the padre at Mission San Luis Rey, was kind, wise, and had a talent for architecture. Father Peyri was at the founding of this mission and remained there for 34 years. Under his leadership, this mission became one of the most successful in Alta California.

San Luis Rey de Francia today

The bells in the campanario of the Pala Asistencia are the original bells that have been rung since 1816. Their simple loud tones ring a clear message to the people.

This statue of San Luis Rey is in the museum of the Pala Asistencia. It was originally at Mission San Luis Rey, but was sent to the Pala Asistencia for safekeeping during secularization. The story tells that bandits tried to steal the statue from Pala. As the bandits tried to drag the statue away, it became heavier and heavier. One bandit became so upset that he shot a bullet into the statue. Finally, the bandits decided to return the statue and suddenly it became lighter in weight. This miracle caused the bandits to run away.

ASISTENCIAS

As more Indians came to the missions, most of the padres found it necessary to plant larger fields of grain. It was also necessary to move the large herds of livestock away from the mission so that more fruits and vegetables could be planted in the mission gardens. Because the large fields and herds were so far away from the mission, the padres had small adobe ranchos built for the Indians who cared for these fields and herds. These small ranchos became known as **asistencias**. A small chapel was built at some of the asistencias so that religious services could be given. Padres would visit these asistencias often and were always pleased when Indians from nearby villages came to the religious services. Many of the padres hoped that these asistencias would become successful missions.

There were twenty or more asistencias in Alta California. Some missions had as many as five. Pala was one of Mission San Luis Rey's asistencias. Father Peyri started Pala as a granary. Later he added an adobe chapel and houses for the Indians. More than a thousand neophytes lived here and the Pala Asistencia was almost a mission by itself.

SANTA INÉS, THE NINETEENTH MISSION

On September 17, 1804, Father Estévan Tápis founded Mission Santa Inés. This mission grew rapidly. The land was good and crops were plentiful. Indians came to the mission and helped to build an adobe church, living quarters, and workshops. Santa Inés was famous for the excellent wood and leather work done by the neophytes. The Indians made beautiful leather saddles. The Santa Inés mission also had a very good hide and tallow industry.

Father Francisco Javier de Uría was kind and generous to the Indians, but a stern teacher. He knew what had to be done at the mission. He designed a water system that brought water underground to the mission, gardens, and orchards. He also designed two water reservoirs to hold extra water. After the earthquake of 1812, Father Uría planned and started a new church. Mission Santa Inés was greatly improved because of Father Uría's ideas and the hard work done by the Indians.

PASQUALA, AN INDIAN GIRL

I am Pasquala, a member of the Tulare Indian tribe. My tribe is very unfriendly to the people who have built missions near the coast.

Once a year my tribe leaves our Indian village and journeys to the ocean. There we catch and dry a year's supply of fish and other sea food to take back to our village in the mountains.

One year I became very ill on the long trip to the ocean. My father tried to give me some herbs that the **shaman** from our tribe often used, but it didn't help. I got sicker! Finally, my father and my mother took me to Santa Inés mission. The padres helped me to get better and my parents decided to be baptized and stay at the mission. We loved the mission.

Each year our tribe of Indians passed by the mission on the way to catch fish at the ocean. They told my mother and father to leave the mission and return to our own village. Finally, one sad day my own tribe came over the hills and killed my father as he was working in the wheat fields. The Indians kidnapped my mother and me and took us back to the Indian village. They punished us for living at the mission.

One night I heard some young Indian men planning to attack the mission. I started on the run to warn the padre at the mission. I ran with all my might and reached Mission Santa Inés just before the raiding party. I was so tired that my heart was nearly bursting, but I had warned the padre in time and the people could protect the mission.

The fighting is over now. I am very tired, but I know I did right to warn the mission padre. I will spend the rest of my days here at the beautiful Mission Santa Inés.

A MISSION HOSPITAL

In December, 1817, Mission San Rafael Arcángel was founded across San Francisco Bay from Mission Dolores. Mission San Rafael Arcángel was started as an asistencia for the many sick Indians at Mission Dolores. At San Rafael there was a warmer climate, lots of sunshine, and the hills protected the mission from the chilly winds.

This asistencia was a long building divided into a chapel, living quarters, and hospital rooms. The padres and the Indians worked hard at this mission and soon some of the sick Indians recovered their health.

After several years, there were hundreds of Indians living at San Rafael. The crops and livestock increased and grain and meat were sent to the San Francisco Presidio.

Mission San Rafael became a full mission in 1823, the twentieth mission.

Mission San Rafael Arcángel

Some of the Indians at Mission Dolores in San Francisco became ill and had to be taken across the bay to Mission San Rafael. The San Rafael mission was started as a hospital asistencia.

As more and more Spanish people came to Alta California, they brought many diseases with them such as chickenpox, measles, smallpox, and mumps. The people who suffered most from these diseases were the Indians. They had no **immunity** to the diseases. For thousands of years the California Indians had depended upon medicine men to help them in times of illness. The medicine men used native herbs and plants to help their patients. These ancient medicines helped or cured the illnesses, but the medicine men could not fight the European diseases. Often it would take only three or four sick people to start an epidemic of chickenpox or measles and thousands upon thousands of Indians would die.

In 1745, the Russians started a company in Kodiak, Alaska to hunt sea otters and seals. In the early 1800's the Russians sailed down the coast of Alta California searching for more sea otters. They built a fort at the site of a Pomo Indian village north of San Francisco Bay. This settlement became known as Fort Ross.

THE LAST LINK IN THE MISSION CHAIN

Young Father José Altimira arrived at Mission Dolores in 1819. He was disappointed by the poor climate and the lack of neophytes at the mission. Father Altimira wanted to put his energy into starting a new mission farther north from the asistencia at San Rafael. He wanted to close Mission Dolores and Mission San Rafael and build a new mission in Sonoma. The padres ignored Father Altimira's plan, so Father Altimira took his idea to the governor of California. Governor Argüello approved of this plan. The governor was worried about Russian settlements at Bodega Bay. Several times the Spanish Army had been sent to Fort Ross to order the Russians to leave California. Governor Argüello felt that a new mission in Sonoma would help to convince the Russians that California belonged to Spain. The governor gave Father Altimira permission to start the new mission in Sonoma.

When the padres heard that Father Altimira had already started building the mission, they were very angry. The padres did not want to close Mission Dolores and Mission San Rafael like Father Altimira had planned. The president of the missions did not want to stop the building of this new mission. He did not want to close Mission Dolores and Mission San Rafael. Finally, it was decided to keep missions at all three locations.

Mission San Francisco Solano at Sonoma was founded by Father Altimira on July 4, 1823. Three hundred Indians came to the new mission from Mission Dolores and other Indians were sent from Mission

San Rafael. Mission Dolores also sent cattle and church goods to the new mission. Even the Russians from nearby Fort Ross sent gifts to this new mission at Sonoma.

Father Altimira and his Indian workers built the mission church of wood. By 1824, there were many mission buildings, orchards, gardens, and vineyards, but the Indians were not happy. Father Altimira was not kind to the Indians and many Indians ran away from the mission to escape his bad temper. It had been fifty-four years since Father Serra had started the first mission in California, and now, Mission San Francisco Solano had become the twenty-first mission and the last mission in the chain.

By July 4th, 1823, twenty-one missions had been founded along the *El Camino Reál*. The Spanish dream had come true. From San Diego to the Golden Gate of San Francisco, the *El Camino Reál* and its missions claimed the land of Alta California for Spain.

Mission San Francisco Solano

* 1. Mission San Diego de Alcalá
* 2. Mission San Carlos Borromeo
  3. Mission San Antonio de Padua
  4. Mission San Gabriel Arcángel
  5. Mission San Luis Obispo de Tolosa
* 6. Mission San Francisco de Asis
  7. Mission San Juan Capistrano
  8. Mission Santa Clara de Asis
  9. Mission San Buenaventura
*10. Mission Santa Barbara
  11. Mission La Purísima Concepción
  12. Mission Santa Cruz
  13. Mission Nuestra Señora de la Soledad
  14. Mission San José
  15. Mission San Juan Bautista
  16. Mission San Miguel Arcángel
  17. Mission San Fernando Rey de España
  18. Mission San Luis Rey de Francia
  19. Mission Santa Inés
  20. Mission San Rafael Arcángel
  21. Mission San Francisco Solano

*Mission with Presidio

Clockwise from upper left, Mission Santa Clara today, Mission San Luis Obispo 1880, the bell tower of Santa Cruz Mission today, Mission Santa Barbara before 1875

BACKTRACKING

1. Why do you think that Mission San José was one of the most successful missions in Northern California?

2. Because of Father Tápis and Father la Cuesta, many Indians came to Mission San Juan Bautista. What did these padres do to bring more Indians to the mission?

3. Mission San Miguel Arcángel had very hot summer months. What were some of the problems caused by the heat?

4. Name three products that were made or grown at Mission San Fernando Rey de España. Where were most of these products sold?

5. Father Peyri was 29 years of age when he came to Mission San Luis Rey de Francia. How old was he when he left the mission?

6. What is an asistencia? Why were asistencias started?

7. At Mission Santa Inés, what was Father Uria famous for?

8. Why was Mission San Rafael Arcángel started?

9. What was Father Altimira's plan when he came to Mission Dolores in San Francisco? Did the other padres like this plan? Why or why not?

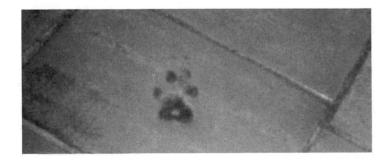

Look carefully at these ladrillos in the Church of Mission San Juan Bautista. Can you see the paw print of the wild animal that stepped on the tile before it was dry? What type of animal do you think made this print? This picture was taken by Jodee Eaton, a fourth grader from Alamo, California. She visited the mission with her class.

In September of 1822, a ship sailed into Monterey Bay flying the Mexican flag. The Spanish flag was taken down from the presidio flag pole where it had been flying ever since Portolá had raised it 53 years before. Now, the Mexican flag flew over all the presidios of Alta California.

CHAPTER FIFTEEN
WHISPERS ALONG THE MISSION TRAIL

CHANGES AT THE MISSIONS

As daily life continued at the twenty-one missions along the *El Camino Reál,* changes were taking place in New Spain. Soon these changes would affect life at the Alta California missions.

The people of New Spain no longer wanted the King of Spain to rule them. They wanted to rule themselves. The people of New Spain fought a **revolution** against the King's soldiers for over ten years. Finally, in 1821, the people of New Spain won their freedom from the King of Spain. Now, the people of New Spain changed the name of their country to Mexico and were able to rule themselves.

The new Mexican government made a law about the California missions and the mission lands. Each mission was to become a church for the people of the nearby pueblos. The mission lands were to be divided between the Indians and Mexican citizens. The padres were no longer to be in charge of the missions or the Indians. This new law called **secularization** would take the mission lands away from the Franciscan padres and the padres would no longer control the land or the Indians of Alta California.

The padres did not like the new Mexican government. Many of the Spanish padres would not sign a paper pledging their loyalty to the Mexican government. The padres did not like the law about secularization of the missions, but they had to obey the law. During the next several years, many of the Spanish padres were forced to leave the missions. They were very sad to go. They loved the Indians and the California missions.

The new Mexican government made a law stating that each mission was to become a church for the people of the nearby pueblos. The padres would no longer be in charge of the missions.

In 1833, the governor of California, Governor Figueroa, tried to divide the lands equally between the Indians and the Mexican citizens. Many of the governor's officials were not honest. They took much of the land for themselves and then began to take the land away from Indian owners. The Indians did not understand the new Mexican laws. Dishonest men cheated them. Often an Indian would put his name on a piece of paper and did not know that he had sold his land. Soon the Indians had no homes, no land, and no animals. Many Indians died from hunger and sickness. Some became servants and worked on the ranchos. A few went to live with their own tribes in the mountains and valleys. The secularization law that was supposed to help the Indians failed miserably and the Indians were left with nothing.

After a few years all the rich mission lands had been taken away from the Indians. Now that the padres and Indians had left the missions there was no one to care for the missions. Many of the beautiful mission churches were left to crumble into ruins.

When the padres and Indians were forced to leave the missions, there was no one to care for the missions. Many of the beautiful mission churches were left to crumble into ruins.

Within a few years, everything that could be carried away from the missions was taken. Statues, bells, fountains, rafters, roof tiles, livestock, plows, carts, and tools disappeared from the missions.

Without rafters and roof tiles, the mission roofs fell and the rain soaked the adobe bricks. Soon the adobe turned into heaps of mud. The bells were silent. The corridors were empty. The gardens and fields where the Indians had worked so hard were overgrown with weeds and shrubs.

Almost one hundred years went by as the mission ruins lay slumbering along the *El Camino Reál*. The footsteps of the busy Indians and Franciscan padres were only lonely whispers of the past.

RESTORATION — NEW LIFE FOR THE MISSIONS!

In the early 1900's people became curious about the mission ruins. Artists began sketching these ruins. When people saw these pictures, many of them wanted to visit the mission sites. Many people planned picnics or family outings at the mission sites and thought about what the missions had been like a **century** before. These visitors heard the lonely whispers echo throughout the mission lands. These whispers stirred the hearts of people and made them want to know more about the missions.

Soon organizations of men and women began exploring old church records and looking for mission foundations along the *El Camino Reál*. With the information they gathered, the **restoration** of the missions began.

Mr. Harry Downie helped to restore many of the California missions. Three of the missions that Mr. Downie helped to restore are Missions San Luis Obispo, San Antonio, and San Carlos Borromeo.

In 1934, the young men of the Civilian Conservation Corps and the National Park Service restored Mission La Puŕisima near Lompoc, California. Gradually, the Civilian Conservation Corps and other organizations began the slow work of restoring the missions. Today, most of the missions have been restored and thousands of people visit them each year.

In 1903, the California Historic Landmarks League selected Mission San Antonio de Padua to be restored. It took four years to finish the restoration of this mission. Forty years later the Hearst Foundation and the Franciscan Fathers of California restored Mission San Antonio again. Because of all the careful hand work done during the last restoration in 1948, Mission San Antonio de Padua is now one of the most beautiful missions in California.

In 1934, the young men of the Civilian Conservation Corps began to restore some of the California missions.

YOU ARE THE EXPLORER

In this book, you have been exploring the New World with many brave explorers. You started your explorations with Columbus in the year 1492, almost 500 years ago! You have sailed up the coast of California with Cabrillo, Vizcaíno, and other famous sailors. You have met the California Indians when they lived in peace and harmony with nature. You have traveled with the Spanish padres and soldiers as they blazed new trails into California. You have watched as the missions were built, one by one, along the *El Camino Reál*.

It is now your turn to explore along the mission trail. As you explore, you will find that each mission has its own special beauty and its own special story.

Be an explorer! Visit a mission! Listen to the whispers! It is up to you to search and find and know about your California heritage!

It is up to you to search and find and know about your California heritage!

Be an explorer! Visit a mission! Listen to the whispers!

BACKTRACKING

1. How did the revolution in New Spain change the lives of the people living there?

2. How did secularization change the missions in Alta California?

3. What happened to the California Indians after secularization?

4. What happened to the California missions after secularization?

5. Why did people become interested in restoring the California missions?

6. Why should you explore along the mission trail? What will you discover?

APPENDIX

ALTA CALIFORNIA MISSIONS

San Diego de Alcalá — July, 1769

San Carlos Borromeo de Carmelo — June, 1770

San Antonio de Padua — July, 1771

San Gabriel Arcángel — September, 1771

San Luis Obispo de Tolosa — September, 1772

San Francisco de Asís — June, 1776

San Juan Capistrano — November, 1776

Santa Clara de Asís — January, 1777

San Buenaventura — March, 1782

Santa Barbara — December, 1786

La Purísima Concepción — December, 1787

Santa Cruz — August, 1791

Nuestra Señora de la Soledad — October, 1791

San José — June, 1797

San Juan Bautista — June, 1797

San Miguel Arcángel — July, 1797

San Fernando Rey de España — September, 1797

San Luis Rey de Francia — June, 1798

Santa Inés — September, 1804

San Rafael Arcángel — December, 1817

San Francisco Solano — July, 1823

FATHER PRESIDENTS IN ALTA CALIFORNIA

Fr. Junípero Serra	1769 – 1784
Fr. Francisco Palóu	1784 – 1785
Fr. Fermín Francisco de Lasuén	1785 – 1803
Fr. Estévan Tápis	1803 – 1812
Fr. José Senan	1812 – 1815
Fr. Mariano Payeras	1815 – 1819
Fr. José Senan	1819 – 1823
Fr. Vicente Francisco Sarría	1823 – 1825
Fr. Narciso Durán	1825 – 1827
Fr. José Bernardo Sanchez	1827 – 1831
Fr. Narciso Durán	1831 – 1838
Fr. José Joaquin Jimeño	1838 – 1844
Fr. Narciso Durán	1844 – 1846

PRESIDIO FOUNDINGS IN ALTA CALIFORNIA

The Presidio of San Diego — July, 1769

The Presidio of Monterey — June, 1770

The Presidio of San Francisco — September, 1776

The Presidio of Santa Barbara — April, 1782

PUEBLO FOUNDINGS IN ALTA CALIFORNIA

San José — November, 1777

Los Angeles — September, 1781

Branciforte (now Greater Santa Cruz) — July, 1797

CREDITS

Tammie Ahlberg, Alamo, CA 94507. Photo page 166

Bancroft Library, University of California, Berkeley, CA 94720. Photo pages 15, 20, 42, 54, 58, 66, 69, 72, 85, 88 (top and bottom), 90, 92, 98, 112, 133, 147 (bottom), 154, 183, 190

Father Virgilio Biasiol, Santa Barbara, CA 93105. Photo page 156

The Robert Bullard Family, Fremont, CA 94539. Photo page 169 (bottom)

California Historical Society, Photographic Archives, 2099 Pacific Avenue, San Francisco, CA 94109. Photo pages 25, 29

Daniel and Katherine Debus, Pleasanton, CA 94566. Cover photo and page 201

Jodee Eaton, Alamo, CA 94507. Photo page 189

Sannie Edgecomb, Danville, CA 94526. Art pages 38, 41, 47, 123, 135, 157

Friends of the Sea Otter and Greenwich Workshop, P.O. Box 221220, Carmel, CA 93922. Photo page 32 by Mort Solberg

Trent and Ryan Kauffman, Alamo, CA 94507. Photo page 199 (top right)

Mark and Susan Leibowitz, Alamo, CA 94507. Photo page 53

Los Angeles County Museum of Natural History, 900 Exposition Blvd., Los Angeles, CA 90007. Photo page 119

Sharon Marocchi, Danville, CA 94526. Music page 135

Mission High School, Eighteenth Street, San Francisco, CA 94114. Title page and pages vi, 45, 130, 209. Paintings by Edith Hamlin, San Francisco, CA 94112

National Aeronautics and Space Administration, Washington, D.C. 20546. Photo pages 1a, 2, 3

Terry Rodriguez, Alamo, CA 94507. Photo page 194

Santa Barbara Mission Archive Library, Father Virgilio Biasiol, O.F.M., Director, Old Mission, Santa Barbara, CA 93105. Photo pages 48, 61, 62 (top), 74 (top and bottom), 79, 81, 87, 91, 101, 111, 118 (bottom), 120, 128, 134 (bottom), 137 (bottom left), 139, 140, 141, 145, 146, 147 (top), 159 (top), 161, 162 (top and bottom), 168, 171, 172 (top), 175 (top), 176, 177 (top), 180, 182, 188 (top right), 188 (bottom left), 193, 195, 197

San Diego de Alcalá Mission Gift Shop, 10818 San Diego Mission Road, San Diego, CA 92108. Photo page 37

San Diego Museum of Man, 1350 El Prado, Balboa Park, San Diego, CA 92101. Photo pages 16, 17

Susan Snyder, Alamo, CA 94507. Photo page 199 (bottom)

Carol Travalini, Alamo, CA 94507. Photo page 11

United States Capitol Building, Washington, D.C. 20515. Photo pages 5, 40, 52

All photos not otherwise credited are the property of Magpie Publications, Copyright © 1986

All illustrations not otherwise credited are the property of Magpie Publications, Copyright © 1986

Production services by Innographics, Burlingame, CA 94010

Printing by Blaco Printers, Inc., San Leandro, CA 94577

GLOSSARY

This glossary gives the meanings of words only as they are used in this book. You may wish to use a dictionary to find other meanings for these words.

alcalde: the mayor of a town or city; an important officer of a town or city.

Alta California: Upper California.

altar: a table or raised area where religious ceremonies are performed.

aqueduct: a ditch, channel, or passage that carries water.

asistencia: an assistant building to a mission where vaqueros and their families lived in order to tend the livestock; an extension or addition to a main part or building.

atolé: a mush made of cornmeal or barley.

Baja California: Lower California.

baptize: to make someone a member of the Christian church by sprinkling or pouring water on them.

barnacles: shellfish that cling to ship bottoms, floating timber, or rocks.

barracks: buildings where soldiers live.

billow: to rise or roll like great waves.

blaze: to make known; to mark.

bless: to make something holy; to protect something from evil.

boisterous: rough and noisy.

caravan: a large group of people traveling together.

caravel: a small ship.

cargo: the freight carried by a ship.

carreta: a cart used for hauling goods, usually pulled by mules or oxen.

cauterize: to close a wound by burning with a hot iron or fire.

century: one hundred years.

chaff: the husks or outer coverings of grains and grasses that have been separated from the seed.

Channel Islands: a group of islands off the coast of Santa Barbara, California.

chant: a song; a short simple song or melody often sung during church services; to sing a short simple melody or song.

chapel: a small church.

characteristic: a special quality, feature, or trait of a person or thing.

chart: a graph, map, or outline showing special facts or conditions; to make a graph or map showing special facts, etc.

Christian: believing in or belonging to the religion of Jesus Christ.

comisionado: a military deputy, usually a sergeant, appointed to supervise the government of a town.

communication: sharing thoughts, ideas, and information by using speech, writing, or sign language.

continent: one of the main land masses on the earth — Europe, Asia, Africa, North America, South America, Australia, and Antarctica.

cosmographer: a person who describes and maps the main features of an area.

crude: rude; rough; poor behavior.

dehydration: loss of water or moisture; to dry out.

devote: dedicated to someone or to doing something; very attached or involved with something.

dialect: a special variety or form of a language; the language of a particular group that differs from the regular language.

diplomat: a person who works well with other people, especially people in government.

drought: dry weather; lack of rain.

ear marked: a mark of identification made on the ear of an animal.

East Indies: islands off the coast of Asia.

El Camino Reál: a road in California built by the Spanish to connect the twenty-one missions; the King's Highway.

epidemic: the spreading of a disease that affects a large number of people.

explorer: a person who searches, investigates, examines, or looks into something carefully for the purpose of discovery.

fabled: does not exist; not real; legendary; fictitious.

faithfulness: to keep a promise or be loyal to someone; trustful; true to one's word.

fanega: a Spanish measurement that equals about 1.6 bushels (about 100 pounds) or about seven acres of land for maize or about 1.75 acres of land for wheat.

ferment: to cause a substance to change by using certain yeasts, molds, bacteria, etc.

fertile: able to produce good crops, such as rich land or soil.

fiesta: a festival or celebration; a religious celebration; a holiday.

fleece: the coat of wool that covers a sheep.

foundation: the base on which a building stands.

founded: to set up, begin, or establish something.

Franciscan: a person who belongs to the religious order that was founded by Saint Francis of Assisi.

game: animals, including birds and fish, that are hunted for food, sport, or profit.

granary: a building for storing grains.

gristmill: a mill for grinding grain.

harmony: agreement; getting along well together; friendliness.

hemp: a fibrous plant; the tough fiber of this plant, used for making coarse fabrics, ropes, etc.

herb: a plant that is used for its flavor or scent and sometimes used in medicine.

home missionary: a person who teaches others who live in his area about his religion.

horizon: the line that forms the boundary between earth and sky; where the earth meets the sky.

humble: poor; lowly; plain; common; without pride.

husk: the dry outside covering of certain seeds, fruits, and vegetables; to remove the dry outside covering of certain seeds, etc.

immunity: protection from a disease; not able to catch a certain disease.

irrigate: to supply land with water by using ditches or canals to carry the water.

irrigation: supplying land with water by using ditches or canals to carry the water.

journal: a daily record or diary of happenings and observations.

kiln: an oven for baking or drying something.

ladrillo: a tile used on floors; a floor tile.

lard: the fat of hogs.

lasso: a long rope or line of hide with a noose (loop) at one end used for roping horses, cattle, etc.

lavandería: a large stone or brick lined basin or pool filled with water and used for washing clothes; a laundry.

limestone: a rock containing calcium carbonate and when heated turns to quicklime.

litter: a framework made of canvas stretched between two poles and used to carry the sick and wounded.

maize: a type of corn.

Majorca: a Spanish island in the Western Mediterranean Sea; the largest of the Balearic Islands.

Manila Galleons: large ships that sailed to Manila, the capital city of the Philippine Islands, from New Spain for purposes of trade.

mayordomo: the foreman or supervisor of a large ranch.

megaphone: a large funnel-shaped object used to talk to a large crowd out or doors or to call to a distance.

mission: a church built to teach religion to the people.

mortar: a mixture such as quicklime, sand, and water that hardens and is used to plaster bricks, stones, or rocks together.

mutiny: a revolt or rebellion against a leader, especially by soldiers or sailors.

nautical: having to do with the sea, ships, sailors, and navigation.

navigational: crossing a sea, ocean, river, etc. in a ship or aircraft; directing the course of a ship or aircraft.

navigator: one who is skilled in directing the course of a ship or aircraft across a sea, ocean, river, etc.; one who explores by sea.

neophyte: a person who is a new member of a church or religion; a new convert; a beginner; newly baptized into a church.

New Albion: An old English name for England.

New World: the continents of North and South America.

official: a person who holds an important office or duty; anything having to do with an important duty, office, or person.

Order of Saint Francis: a religious group that was founded by Saint Francis of Assisi.

padre: a priest; Christian minister; Catholic priest.

patio: an area usually attached to a house used for outdoor living; an inner courtyard.

permanent: lasting; unchanged; not temporary.

pestle: a club-shaped hand tool usually made of stone or wood used to mash or grind seeds, grains, herbs, etc.

plain: flat or level ground; clear, open area.

plaster: a mixture of quicklime, sand, and water that hardens when dry and is used to cover walls, ceilings, etc.

plow: a tool used to turn the soil and dig small ditches so seeds or seedlings can be planted; to dig or turn the soil.

plunder: to rob; steal.

pobladores: settlers; founders.

possession: belonging to a person; ownership.

presidio: a fort; military outpost.

produce: fruits and vegetables; products from crops, gardens, and orchards.

pueblo: a town; village.

quadrangle: a square space or courtyard surrounded by buildings; the buildings that are around a square space or courtyard.

quench: to put an end to, such as thirst; to put out or stop; to cool.

quicklime: a white powder from baked limestone used in mortar and plaster.

raid: a sudden attack; to attack.

reata: a leather rope used to tie or lasso cattle, sheep, etc.

relocate: to move to another place or area.

rendezvous: a meeting; a place for a meeting, especially ships or troops.

represent: to stand for something, such as a word or symbol; to speak or act for someone else.

representative: a person who speaks or acts for another person; an agent or deputy.

reservoir: a place where water is collected and stored for use.

responsible: trusted; capable of completing a task; accountable; answerable.

restoration: bringing back to a normal condition or use; reconstruction of an old building showing it in its original state.

revolution: the overthrow of a government; a complete change in something.

rheumatism: a disease in which there is stiffness in the muscles and joints, making movement painful.

rigging: the ropes and chains used to support the masts, sails, etc. on a ship.

route: a way or road for travel; the way or road traveled.

rugged: rocky; hilly; a difficult passage or route.

scurvy: a disease that causes swollen and bleeding gums, weak muscles, spots on the skin, great weakness, etc. due to a diet lacking vitamin C.

sea otter: a fur-bearing sea mammal with webbed feet for swimming and a long tail living along the Pacific Coast of the North American continent.

secularization: to separate something from its religious connection; to take something away from the church; to make something nonreligious.

seedling: a small plant or tree; grown from a seed; a tree not yet three feet high.

seize: to grab or grasp suddenly with force; to suddenly take control of something.

shaman: a type of Indian doctor or medicine man.

sickle: a curved tool with a hooklike blade and a short handle used for cutting grain, grass, etc.

siesta: a midday or afternoon rest or nap.

sinew: a cord or tough white tissue that connects a muscle with a bone; a tendon.

site: the position of a building or town; the area on which something is located.

slaughter: the killing or butchering of cattle, sheep, etc. for food.

stockade: a fence-like barrier or enclosure built for protection and made of strong posts, timbers, or stakes placed upright in the ground.

Strait of Anián: an imaginary water passageway that was supposed to connect the Pacific and Atlantic Oceans.

Strait of Magellan: a narrow passage of water at the tip of South America founded by the explorer Magellan and connecting the Atlantic and Pacific Oceans.

tallow: the fatty tissue or hard fat of cattle, sheep, etc. that is melted and used to make candles, soap, etc.

teja: a tile used on roofs; a rooftile.

temporary: not permanent; not lasting or existing for a very long time; lasting for a short time.

thresh: to separate the grains or seeds from wheat stalks by beating or stomping.

tortilla: a thin, round cake made from cornmeal and baked on a hot flat pan.

Trade Winds: winds that blow in one regular course or continually in the same direction.

unison: two or more voices or tones singing or playing together at the same pitch.

vaccine: a virus used as protection against diseases such as smallpox, measles, mumps, polio, etc.

vaquero: a cowboy; a herdsman.

vat: a large container for liquids.

venison: the meat of a deer or similar animal.

vestment: clothing like a robe or gown usually used in religious ceremonies; ceremonial clothing used by a priest, minister, etc.

viceroy: a person appointed by a king or other leader to rule a country or province

vineyard: a large area planted with grapevines that produce grapes for winemaking.

volunteer: a person who offers to do something without being asked; a person who enters into any service of his own free will.

weary: very tired; exhausted; fatigued.

winnow: to remove the chaff or outer covering from grain by means of wind or a current of air.

yoke: a wooden frame fitting the head and shoulders of an ox or other animal used for pulling carts, plows, etc.; a frame fitting over the top of a bell from which the bell is hung.

PRONUNCIATION GUIDE

Acapulco (Ah-kah-PULL-koh)

alcalde (ahl-KAHL-day)

Altimira, José (Ahl-tah-MEER-ah, Hoh-SAY)

Anián, Strait of (Ah-NEE-an, Straight of)

Anza, Juan Bautista de (ON-zah, Wan Bah-TEES-ta de)

Argüello (Ar-GWAY-yo)

asistencia (ah-sis-TEN-see-ah)

atolé (ah-toh-LAY)

Bouchard, Hipolito (Boo-sharr, Hip-oh-LEE-toh)

Cabrillo, Juan Rodríguez (Cah-BREE-yoh, Wan Roh-DREE-gez)

Cambón (Kam-BONE)

carreta (kar-RET-tah)

Cavaller, José (Kav-ah-YAIR, Hoh-SAY)

Cermenho, Rodríguez (Ser-MEN-hoh, Roh-DREE-gez)

Columbus, Christopher (Koh-LUM-bus, KRIS-toh-fur)

Comisionado (ko-mee-see-oh-NAH-doh)

Crespí (Kress-PE)

El Camino Reál (El Kah-MEE-noh Ree-AL)

El Pueblo de Nuestra Señora de Los Angeles (El PWEB-loh day New-AY-strah Seen-YOR-ah day Lohs AHN-hay-lace)

El Pueblo de San José de Guadalupe (El PWEB-loh day San Hoh-SAY day Gwah-dah-LOO-pay)

Fages (FAH-hace)

fanega (fan-AY-gah)

Ferrelo, Bartolomé (Fair-ELL-oh, Bar-toh-loh-MAY)

Fiesta (fee-ESS-tah)

Figueroa (Fee-gair-ROH-ah)

Font, Pedro (Font, PAY-droh)

Gálvez, José de (GAL-vez, Ho-SAY day)

Garcés (Gar-SAYS)

Guadalupe (Gwah-dah-LOO-pay)

Ibañez, Florencio (EE-bohn-ez, Flor-INN-see-oh)

Juana Maria (HWAN-ah Mah-REE-yah)

ladrillos (lah-DREE-yohs)

La Purísima Concepción (Lah Pur-EE-see-mah Cone-sep-SEE-own)

Lasuén, Fermín Francisco de (Lah-SWAIN, Fair-MEAN Frahn-CEES-koh day)

lavandería (lah-vahn day-REE-ah)

Magellan, Ferdinand (Mah-JELL-an, FUR-dih-nand)

maize (MAYS)

Majorca (May-YOUR-kah)

Mendoza (Men-DOH-zah)

Mohave (Moh-HAH-vee)

Murguía, José (Mer-GWEE-yah, Hoh-SAY)

Navidad (Nah-vee-DAHD)

neophyte (NEE-oh-fight)

Neve, Felipe de (NEV, Feh-LEEP day)

Nuestra Señora de la Soledad (New-AY-strah Seen-YOR-ah day lah Soh-leh-DAHD)

Palóu (Pah-LOO)

Pasquala (Pass-KWAL-lah)

patio (PAH-tee-oh)

Peralta, Luis María (Pair-AHL-tah, Loo-EES Mah-REE-ah)

Peralta, María Loreto Alviso (Pair-AHL-tah, Mah-REE-ah Lor-EE-toh Al-VEE-soh)

Pérez (Pair-EZZ)

Peyri, Antonio (PAY-ree Ahn-TOHN-ee-oh)

pobladores (poh-blah-DOR-race)

Portolá, Gaspár de (Por-toh-LAH, Gas-PAR day)

pueblo (PWEB-loh)

Ramirez, José (Rah-MEER-ez, Hoh-SAY)

reata (ray-AH-tah)

reservoirs (REZ-er-vores)

Reyes, Francisco (RAYS, Frahn-SEES-coh)

Ripoll (Re-POLE)

Rivera (Ree-VAIR-ah)

San Antonio de Padua (San An-TOH-nee-oh day PAH-doo-wah)

San Buenaventura (San BWAY-nah-ven-TOOR-ah)

San Carlos Borromeo de Carmelo (San KARR-lohs BORE-oh-MAY-oh day Kar-MELL-oh)

San Diego de Alcalá (San Dee-AY-goh day Al-cahl-AH)

San Fernando Rey de Espana (San Fair-NON-doh Ray day Ess-POHN-yah)

San Francisco de Asís (San Frahn-SIS-koh day Ah-SEECE)

San Francisco Solano (San Frahn-SIS-koh Sew-LAH-noh)

San Gabriel Arcángel (San GAY-bree-ell Ark-AIN-jell)

San Juan Bautista (San Wan Bah-TEES-tah)

San José (San Hoh-SAY)

San Juan Capistrano (San Wan Kap-is-TRON-oh)

San Luis Obispo de Tolosa (San Loo-EES Oh-BEES-poh day Toh-LOH-sah)

San Luis Rey de Francia (San Loo-EES Ray day FRONK-ee-uh)

San Miguel Arcángel (San Mee-GELL Ark-AIN-jell)

San Rafael Arcángel (San Rah-fah-ELL Ark-AIN-jell)

Santa Barbara (SAHN-tah BAR-bah-rah)

Santa Clara de Asís (SAHN-tah KLAIR-ah day Ah-SEECE)

Santa Cruz (SAHN-tah KROOZ)

Santa Inés (SAHN-tah Ee-NEZ)

Sarria, Vicente Francisco de (Sar-EE-uh, Vih-SEN-tee Frahn-SIS-koh day)

Serra, Junipero (SAIR-ah, Hoo-NIP-er-oh)

Siesta (See-ESS-tah)

Soldados de Cuera (Sohl-DAH-dohs
   day Koo-AIR-ah)

Somera (Sew-MAIR-ah)

Strait of Anián (Straight of
   Ah-NEE-an)

Tápis, Estévan (TAP-eez,
   Ess-TAY-von)

tejas (TAY-hahs)

Vanegas, José (Van-AY-gahs,
   Hoh-SAY)

vaqueros (vah-CARE-ohs)

Vara (VAIR-ah)

Vila (VEE-lah)

Vizcaíno, Sebastián
   (Viz-cah-EE-noh,
   Seh-BASS-tee-an)

INDEX

214

216